CREATURES OF THE SAME GOD

CREATURES
of the
SAME GOD

Explorations in
Animal Theology

ANDREW LINZEY

Lantern Books • New York
A Division of Booklight Inc.

2009
LANTERN BOOKS
128 Second Place
Brooklyn, NY 11231
www.lanternbooks.com

First Published in Great Britain in 2007 by The Winchester University Press, University of Winchester, Winchester SO22 4NR, England, ISBN: 978-1-906113-00-1

Printed in the United States of America

LIBRARY OF CONGRESS CATALOGING-IN-PUBLICATION DATA

Linzey, Andrew.
  Creatures of the same God : explorations in
animal theology / Andrew Linzey.
     p. cm.
  Originally published: Winchester, England :
Winchester University Press, 2007.
  ISBN-13: 978-1-59056-142-3 (alk. paper)
  ISBN-10: 1-59056-142-2 (alk. paper)
  1. Animals—Religious aspects—Christianity.
  2. Animal welfare—Religious aspects—Christianity.
  I. Title.
  BT746.L58 2009
  241'.693—dc22
                                    2009009868

For Priscilla Cohn

Philosopher and animal advocate, whose work for animals has been an inspiration

Contents

Introduction

"They're Only Animals—For Heaven's Sake!"

"I don't know why you're spending all your time on this. They're only animals—for heaven's sake!" That was the reaction of one of my fellow students at King's College, London, when I was studying theology in the 1970s. It was not, it has to be said, an uncommon reaction. Many of my contemporaries had enormous difficulty in understanding why the cause of animals fascinated me, and why I felt compelled at an early age to work for animal protection. Neither was this reaction limited to fellow students. The Dean of King's, Sydney Evans—in many ways an inspiring and courageous man to whom my own debt is vast—could not help quipping on one occasion that "Andrew will make a fine priest—if only he can get these animals out of his system!"

It was not, I think, pure stubbornness that made me continue. I was genuinely interested to know how my fellow ordinands and my illustrious teachers could justify what I regarded as dismissive and negligent attitudes toward God's other creatures. Specifically, how could they justify eating meat when there were plenteous alternatives? Back then, it must be said, there were not many vegetarians (I was the only one in a university hall of 200 or so) and they found my conscience-pricking rather irritating, and said so. I suppose I was, for them, just another student obsessed with a particular issue.

Looking back, however, I think they did me a favor—without knowing it. For I was forced to consider—more than I would have in congenial company—the rational grounds for thinking animals mattered and that theology should properly take account of them.

Of course, animals were not just an intellectual issue. Looking back through the mists of time, I recall some distinctly religious experiences in my teens—when I was only fourteen years old to be precise. These experiences opened my mind to the idea of a Creator and that caring for other living things was a Christian duty. My parents were not strongly religious at the time and when I announced at that youthful age that I wanted to be a priest, it not unnaturally provoked some incredulity, even mirth. In the same year, I became a vegetarian, which—for family and friends—was even more vexing.

Later, when I was studying at University College, Cardiff, I started writing a book in an attempt to work out my position more fully. What began as a kind of part-time hobby was finally completed during my last year of theological training at St. Augustine's College, Canterbury—the place that was previously the college of the Anglican Communion. Among other things, I recall praying in the chapel surrounded by plaques commemorating the names and dates of previous students who had gone out as missionaries to the ends of the earth and met unfortunate ends. It was an inspiring, if rather daunting, environment in which to contemplate one's future ministry.

My book *Animal Rights: A Christian Assessment* (SCM Press, 1976) came out when I was a curate in Dover. And it caused something of a storm. Elsewhere I have given some account of this[1] but, suffice to say, the book touched a nerve. It came out just before Peter Singer's *Animal Liberation* in the UK and coincided with a great deal of rethinking about the status of animals by philosophers. Thirty years ago, the whole notion of animal rights was something of a novelty, and it is fair to say that I felt like a lone voice crying in the wilderness. Since then, of course, the movement for the rights of animals has become a worldwide phenomenon. The attention that my book received meant that the die was effectively cast—though I hardly knew it at the time. The invitations to write and talk about animals have increased ever since, with the consequence that I have been thinking, writing, teaching, and preaching about animals and Christianity for almost all my adult life.

Why bother, then, with animals? "They're only animals—for heaven's sake!" It is a question deserving of an answer.

In the first place, the rational case for animals is infinitely stronger than many suppose. Reason has its limits of course, and I have already indicated that that is not where my convictions originated. But, in purely intellectual terms, the case for treating animals better than we do is one of the strongest I have encountered in ethics. Let me make the point as simply as possible. Given that it is reasonable to suppose (as reasonable as almost anything is) that mammals (at least) experience pain and suffering only to a greater or lesser extent than we do, then the infliction of suffering and death upon them merits strong (some would say very strong) justification. To kill or inflict suffering without justification is wrong. Now that is surely a fairly minimal position in ethics, and not many would want to dissent from it.

But consider: we routinely kill and inflict suffering on millions, if not billions, of animals in the world today. In some cases there may be genuine need, but in the vast majority of cases there is nothing of the sort. To take one issue, consider the routine harm we cause animals in sporting pursuits, such as sport hunting, including bird shooting, coursing, cockfighting and bull-baiting (still legal in some countries), bullfighting, rodeos, and the use of animals in circuses. None of these practices could remotely be called "necessary" in the sense of being unavoidable or essential for human health and well-being. Pleasure does not constitute moral necessity.

If tomorrow we decided only to desist from killing and causing suffering for sport and entertainment, the world would be significantly better for animals. Even this we have failed to achieve. In some countries, cruel sports (or some of them) are prohibited, but not in most. And do not forget: we are considering here practices that offend the most basic and minimal of ethical standards. Even if the reader only agrees with me about this *one* issue, there is here a huge agenda for moral reform worldwide. I would love to see even just a part of this goal achieved before I die.

Secondly, although Christianity has a poor record on animals (as it does, it must be said, on the treatment of slaves, women, children, and gays), it is also the case that Christian theology, when creatively and critically handled, can provide a strong basis for animal rights. Consider the relevance of some basic Christian positions, such as the idea that animals are fellow creatures. This means, minimally, that they have some God-given value in themselves. They do not have value just in relation to us, but to their Creator. It follows that to regard them and treat them just as things, commodities, or resources is a spiritually impoverished understanding of their status.

Now I know Christians have often viewed animals like that, but so they have in the case of slaves, and arguably women as well. Consider further: animals have a God-given life (*nephesh* in Hebrew). This means, among other things, that each individual animal is animated by the same Holy Spirit that gives life to all creatures, humans included. This bestows on sentient life especially capacities for living—capacities for feeling, capacities for seeing—unique and distinct potentialities, which must logically be valued by their Creator. God has created a multi-eyed and multi-feeling world that is, as it were, felt by the Spirit *from within*.² Consider yet further: humans have "dominion" over animals. But that "dominion" (*radah* in Hebrew) does not mean despotism, rather we are set over creation to care for what God has made and to treasure God's own treasures.

In these very basic ways, and many others, Christian theology can and should challenge our relentless exploitation of animals. But where are the theologians who articulate these basic insights among others? There are some, and I have (I hope generously) drawn attention to their work throughout the book. But there are simply not enough of them. What I have had to face—and what incidentally drives me on—is the sad realization that unless I represent these ideas, they will (more often than not) go unarticulated. This recognition gives me no pride or pleasure. I would happily, sometimes more than happily, have vacated my role as an animal theologian, if there were others prepared to take my place. Thankfully, there are now more than a handful who are working on these

issues worldwide, but whereas philosophical work on animals
has increased apace over the last thirty years, I fear theology
is—in the words attributed to William Temple—"still in its
infancy" when it comes to animals.

People sometimes say to me: "But why this issue, Andrew,
when there are so many others?" Well, in point of fact, I *am*
concerned about other issues. I have written, for example,
on the rights of children, on war and violence, on research
on embryos, and on justice for gays.[3] I am deeply concerned
about a range of moral issues. The theoretical position I hold
in ethics, namely that the weak and the vulnerable make a
special claim upon us, has wide implications. But it is a bit
rich when people call me a "single issue man" when—in aca-
demia—people are lauded for spending their life studying
"single issues," like the Old or New Testaments, Christian
doctrine, or Church history, and never have to endure the
same reproach. Why should "animals" be regarded as a "single
issue" when, in fact, considering our obligations toward them
involves acquiring knowledge of biology, history, law, philosophy, theology, and ethics, and has direct moral relevance to
literally millions of other species? It is all part of our academic
myopia that studying the lives and welfare of non-human creatures in the world should be designated as a "single issue." To
give just one example, only last summer I spent days learning
about the ecology of harp and hood seals in order to understand the terrible injuries (and terrible they are) inflicted by
the annual Canadian seal hunt.[4]

Thirdly, what has also driven me on is the recognition
that the problems with which I wrestle have massive practical implications for how humans live on the planet, as well
as for how animals are treated. Not many people, certainly
not many academics, have the privilege of writing and saying things that have direct relevance to the lives of others.
I am well aware that if I had confined myself in Oxford to
writing some highly technical papers on some limited aspects
of biblical or doctrinal understandings of animals, published
in some select but obscure journals, that I would have more
readily earned the respect of my colleagues. Doubtless, that
work needs to be done, and should be done, and is meritori-

ous. But the issues are so pressing and—in terms of suffering alone—so urgent, that I have felt compelled to engage a
wider readership, and articulate positions that have involved
me in no little controversy.

Much as I would love to be loved and respected by all my
colleagues, I do not for a moment seriously regret having
challenged for example the "patenting" and cloning of animals in biomedical research, the hunting of animals for sport,
the treatment of animals in fur farming, the Canadian seal
hunt, and the need to kill for food. In the absence of the testimony of others, I have felt compelled to articulate theological
positions that challenge our easygoing acceptance of animal
exploitation. Someone who has engaged these and similar
issues in the public arena cannot expect anything other than
misperception and mistreatment at the hands of the media. As
I used to say to my ethics students preparing for ordination,
there are only two ways to deal with the media: either elect
to take the Buddha's vow of eternal silence, or make one's
voice known as responsibly as one humanly can, and take the
consequences.

And yet, there are aspects of the current "animal movement" (for want of a better term) that do cause me disquiet,
and which I have also variously drawn attention to in this book.
The first is the self-righteousness that afflicts all campaigners,
and animal ones in particular. This will be a familiar theme to
fellow advocates for animals who have heard me speak at one
meeting or another during the past two decades. As I see it,
we are in a mess when it comes to animals. As I have repeat-
edly said: there is no pure land. Our exploitation of animals
is so massive and relentless that it is impossible for anyone
to say that they are not party to this exploitation, directly or
indirectly, either through the products we buy, the clothes
we wear, or the taxes we pay. Extricating ourselves from this
exploitation should be our aim, but its absolute practical realization in our individual and social lives is currently beyond
us. Even those who are vegan (and who desist from all products and by-products of slaughter) have to face the problem
that their food comes from crops that are sustained only by
the ruthless killing of competitor species. There is hardly a

substance in the world—from fire extinguisher substances to soybeans—that has not been tested on animals.[5]

That is why I have persistently argued for a strategy of personal and social "progressive disengagement from injury to animals"[6]—a strategy that involves each of us going as far as we can toward realizing the goal of living a cruelty-free and violence-free life. But we must realize that not all people are able to move at the same pace, and that many of us are deeply attached in one form or another to the benefits of animal exploitation. We need to provide therapy and counsel to those who want to take steps toward a less exploitative world. They need and deserve encouragement and help. Self-righteous postures, however, are inappropriate and humanly counterproductive. We are all sinners when it comes to animals. That recognition should inform a less strident, more compassionate form of campaigning. Those who confront others and say, "It's veganism or nothing," will often have gained precisely "nothing" for the animals.

Elsewhere, I have had the temerity to propose to fellow advocates that:

> We need a similar Truth and Reconciliation Commission concerning animals [to that chaired by Archbishop Desmond Tutu in South Africa]. We need to provide space and opportunity in the animal movement for people to confess the truth, to repent, to be accepted, and be forgiven. I make no apology for the use of the term "forgiveness." We all desperately need forgiveness. Above all else, what puts people off our movement is the creeping self-righteousness that sadly attends almost all progress movements as a matter of course. But self-righteousness is a killer of moral sensibility and practical progress.
>
> For myself, I have much to confess. I used to enjoy eating meat. As a teenager, I went fishing. I used to "love" animals so much that I used to collect them in cages in my garden; foolishly and ludicrously I used to think they enjoyed my company. Even now I have a daily struggle with veganism, and I'm not all there yet—and I assure you, that's not all of it. . . . I foray into all of this because I am convinced that the liberation of animals is also human liberation. Just as women's liberation is also

about liberating men from unjust and oppressive attitudes, so too is animal liberation. . . . Perhaps we need a new organization like "AA" but called "AAA"—Animal Abusers Anonymous. I would gladly join. The truth will convict us all.[7]

The second cause of disquiet—and, to be frank, distress, trauma, and tears—is that some animal rights people are now adopting violent tactics. One example sticks in my mind. A UK TV Channel 4 program titled *The Rise and Rise of the Animal Rights Movement*, broadcast in 2001, comprised an interview with Andrew Blake of the organization Disabled for Animal Research. Barely restraining his tears, he read some of the hate letters and death threats he had received. I know Andrew because I have debated with him on television, and I believe that he is seriously mistaken in regarding animal research as a panacea for human illness, including his own. But he is, I believe, a sincere man acting according to his conscience.

It was nothing less than humiliating to discover that people who similarly oppose animal research would resort to such cruel tactics.[8]

Violent tactics, including threats, intimidation, arson, destruction of property, and the rest, are utterly counterproductive and must be resolutely opposed. Although they are performed only by a tiny minority, they give the media an easy excuse to label the whole movement as anti-human, fanatical, and violent. In the process, of course, it is violence—not animal suffering—that becomes the issue. The vast majority of animal rights people are tarred with the same brush, and great swathes of otherwise sympathetic people are alienated from the goals of the humane movement. I have heard it suggested that militant animal rights people are like the suffragettes, but the comparison is more revealing than is appreciated. A new study has shown how counterproductive violence was as a tactic for that movement as well.[9]

But I do not oppose violence simply because it is counterproductive. I oppose it because it betrays animal rights philosophy. Those who resort to such tactics really have not understood that animal rights is about the extension of moral concern to all sentient beings—humans obviously included.

One cannot get to animal rights by trampling on human ones. In an article in the animal rights magazine *The Animals' Agenda*, I spelled out in unambiguous terms the kind of self-contradiction involved in resorting to violence:

> To sanction such violence is to adopt the ethics of the vivisector who justifies the infliction of harm in the hope of a greater good. . . . I believe that our movement is facing a Rubicon. If animal rights are not to become synonymous with terror tactics, individuals and organizations must move, and move fast, to dissociate themselves completely from violent militancy. . . . During the last 30 years, our movement has, despite many setbacks, enjoyed outstanding success. But the ultimate success of our cause is not inevitable or inexorable. It has been said that ours is not a cause to win, ours is a cause to lose. I believe it. But we shall not only lose, we shall deserve to lose, if we fail to break free of the taint of terror tactics. It is nothing less than tragic that a movement that contains so many honourable and conscientious people should be publicly held to ransom by a small group of violent zealots. . . . I beg my fellow peaceable animal advocates to take their stand now, as a matter of urgency, before others take their stand against us.[10]

Written as it was before the terrorist attacks on 11 September 2001, it could not, sadly, have been more prophetic.

As I see it, then, animal people need to pursue their goals without self-righteousness and always, without exception, in a peaceful, civilized manner. And also, I believe they must keep within the law. Years ago, I remember seeing a slogan painted on a building: "Animal Liberation" with the letter "A" in a circle above it—which I believe is an anarchist symbol. Without appreciating it, the sloganizers had indicated their own self-contradiction. For anarchists believe in the rejection of the rule of law and all coercive authority. But animals, above all, need law. The best justification of law is that it defends the weakest and the defenseless. And what animal people are working toward, among other things, is the embodiment of protection for animals in law. The adoption of anarchism worldwide would allow even more cruelty and abuse of animals. It makes no sense for animal protectionists of all people to undermine law. While not everything depends upon the enactment of law, the creation of civilized laws is absolutely essential in order to make progress.

Some people reading this might reply: "Well, you have been unrelentingly critical of the animal movement both in word and in print. Why, then, do you go on supporting it?" The simple answer is that we are—and should be—most critical of the things we love. I believe it was the poet Stephen Spender who once said of the author and critic George Orwell that he was ferociously committed to socialism and ferociously critical of it. Commitment and criticism go together, or should do. The best analogy I can provide is my commitment to the Christian Church. I love the Church of England in many ways, but am deeply critical of its frequent betrayal (as I see it) of the Christian Gospel, including its lack of concern about animals. It is as difficult for me to remain a part of the animal movement as it is for me to remain a member of the Church of England. Both infuriate me at times, even provoke despair, not to mention tears, but I do not intend to abandon them.

Years ago, I thought half-jestingly that I might start the "Linzey Church," comprising people who unambiguously share my own moral vision of the world. But, as I reflected more seriously, I began to realize that there would be only one member: myself. Unless we are to resign the human race entirely, we have no choice but to go on working within compromised institutions that sometimes betray their own deepest values. I belong to a Christian Church that has sanctioned violence and immense cruelty in the course of its history, but always such actions have been contrary (though many have not seen it) to its Gospel of love—in the same way I remain part of the animal movement whose supporters sometimes also betray its core values.

Perhaps naïvely, I have a continuing faith in the civilizing power of ideas. I have seen with my own eyes how students can, at best, respond to new ideas and be changed by them. It was said of the poet T. S. Eliot that to him a new idea was an experience. Intellectual openness, doubtless, is not the most heroic of the virtues, but it is one to which I remain committed on a daily basis. In that regard, the establishing of the Oxford Centre for Animal Ethics is a landmark event. The aim is to create an international and multi-disciplinary center at Oxford dedicated to the ethical enhancement of the status of animals through academic research, teaching, and publication. It acts as an independent "think tank" for the advancement of progressive thought about animals. It is the first center of its kind in the world, and I am proud to have founded it.

It is vital that universities provide the means of rational engagement with the animal issue. The Centre aims to do just that—and in the process show how rational debate is the best, perhaps the only, answer to violence and illegality. Academics and researchers of all disciplines (both in the sciences and the humanities) are eligible to become affiliated as fellows of the Centre, and graduate students as associate fellows. The Centre will be the hub of an international network of academics that will collaborate and exchange views via the web and electronic communication. After years of apparent neglect, it is heartening to see signs that animals are at last beginning to be taken seriously—by the theological community especially. The enquiries and invitations that I receive from students (many of them doing dissertations in the subject or studying the issue as part of their courses in ethics) provide evidence of growing interest. Animals are, at last, beginning to figure on the intellectual agenda. Animal people need, most of all, to invest in the power of their ideas and in rational discussion. Like Christians, they need to move from trying to program the truth to putting truth on the program.

The essays collected here represent some of my work in the area of animals and theology since my *Animal Theology* was published in 1994, and its evangelical sequel *Animal Gospel* in 1999. Each essay addresses a particular topic and tries to take the reader a little further. All have been revised or reworked to avoid repetition, though the final chapter ("Towards a Prophetic Church for Animals") acts as a summing-up and touches on many of the previous points. A short preface to each piece indicates its genesis and the intended audience.

Various people have made this book possible. My chief thanks are due to Professor Elizabeth Stuart of the University of Winchester, who generously supported the manuscript and made publication possible. Professor Stuart has an international reputation as a scholar and a pioneer in theology and ethics, and it has been a special pleasure to work with her in the editing and production side of the book. It is a great honor to have one of the first books—if not the very first book—published by the new Winchester University Press. Dr. Philip Kennedy of Mansfield College, Oxford and Professor Mark Rowlands of the University of Miami kindly read the entire manuscript and made painstaking and insightful comments. I am happy to record my debt to my wife, Jo, for her help with editing. Myra Wilkinson copyedited the book with great skill and care. Needless to say, responsibility for any errors remains entirely my own.

My overwhelming concern has been for accessibility more than anything else. I am increasingly frustrated by theological works that hide behind a sophistication of language whereby the argument proceeds, if at all, by oblique and frequently obtuse references. I have dared to call a spade a spade, whilst also allowing necessary space for the development of the argument. My hope is that this book will reach and encourage the new generations of students who are now wrestling with these topics as never before. People are welcome to contact me at andrewlinzey@aol.com.

Andrew Linzey
Oxford Centre for Animal Ethics
Michaelmas 2006

Religion and Sensitivity to Animal Suffering

This opening chapter addresses the ambiguity of religious per-
spectives on animals. Some kinds of religious vision can help
energize individuals to work for the protection of animals, but
others can become the means whereby human beings sustain
their own self-interest. As I see it, the challenge for almost all
world religions is to find ways of relating the best of their ethi-
cal teachings to the newly emerging movement of sensitivity
to animals. The chapter is a revised version of an address to
the first UK Interfaith Celebration of Animals organized by the
World Congress of Faiths and held at Golders Green Unitarian
Church, 13 June 2004. It was first published in Interreligious
Insight, *3/3 (July 2005).*

One World: One People: One Human Family. To this larger
vision we are being urged to respond by both the disasters and
the discoveries that distinguish this our time. No longer can
place be found for tribalisms, racialisms, sectarianisms, funda-
mentalisms. What God would seem to be saying through the
turbulence and tragedies is that we must all learn to acknowledge and accept each other across old barriers and explore
new ways of living together without losing what is distinctive
and humanly good in our different cultures.

The words are from a sermon by Sydney Evans preached at
the Inauguration of the Third General Synod of the Church
of England in 1980.[1] The underlying vision of "universal ecu-
menism," of the unity of all humankind, which informs much

interfaith dialogue, remains deeply prophetic. But there is a larger, wider vision still—not just of human unity, but also the unity of all life, of all living creatures.

It was anticipated, at least to a degree, by the founder of the World Congress of Faiths, Sir Francis Younghusband. Recounting one of his mystical experiences, he writes of how he "felt in touch with the flaming heart of the world. What was glowing in all creation and in every single human being was a joy far beyond mere goodness, as the glory of the sun is beyond the glow of a candle. A mighty joy-giving Power was at work in the world—at work in all about me and at work in every living thing."[2]

Younghusband's attitude is essentially one of celebration of all those other creatures who share this planet with us. But some might legitimately question whether we have much, if anything, to celebrate. Almost everywhere, they might say, we have abused animals, cruelly treated them for sport, or profit, or our own advantage. What have we to celebrate when our record is so dismal? But it may be that our record is so dismal because we have lost the capacity to celebrate, the capacity for wonder, awe, and astonishment at the marvelous creatures around us. Perhaps we only think of animals as things here for us, or for our own advantage, because we have not ever seen them as subjects of value in their own right.

If we do not have any sense of what Younghusband meant when he spoke of the "mighty joy-giving Power . . . at work in every living thing," then we should not be surprised if humans go on living mean, narrow, selfish, essentially exploitative lives. As I have written elsewhere, "The central point is that celebration involves the recognition of worth, of value, outside ourselves. Human beings are not the sum total of all value; outside of ourselves there is something—and someone—to discover."[3]

That is the first great theme of much religious teaching: the celebration of life. The second is reverence for life. "Reverence" means more than just "respect." The German term *Ehrfurcht* used by Albert Schweitzer has a mystical or religious connotation meaning a claim made upon one.[4] Reverence denotes an experience of value that engenders humility.

To have reverence is to acknowledge that a greater power than ourselves, a life-giving power, is at work in the universe; that we all come from the same creative hand, and we all share a common gift of life. This sense of fellow-feeling, of kinship, of "creatureliness," is what we desperately need to recover in our dealings with animals.

Frequently, religious people speak of the specialness of human beings, how we are made in the image of God, or blessed by the Spirit; but so often they fail to point out the equal truth that humans are also the most unlovely species in the world—the species capable of degrading itself beyond that of any other creature. Unique we may be, but unique also is our violence, our wickedness, our capacity for evil. Alone among all beings in the universe we are capable of the best—and also the very worst.

We have to rediscover a sense of humility. So often we have thought that our power over animals is its own self-justification. But there is, as Younghusband recognized, another Power—a "mighty joy-giving Power" by which we are sustained, and by which, some of us believe, we will ultimately be judged. The more adequate—and certainly more biblical—view is not that we are the "master species" but the "servant species"[5]—the one species uniquely commissioned to care for the earth and its inhabitants.

The third theme is compassion for life. Philosopher William James wrote of how religion is the oxygen of morality. Faith creates moral energy because it kindles the sense of what he terms "an infinite demander's sake" as opposed to a situation where "there are none but finite demanders."[6]

Certainly compassion does not come easily to the human species. It requires all the resources that religion can provide for its survival. We need a capacity to feel for others, to imagine their suffering, to act altruistically, even against our own perceived self-interest. That is why religious vision—a vision of more than ourselves—is so pivotal to how we treat other species.

Theologian Jonathan Edwards once described sin as a kind of shrinkage. He writes how sin, "like some powerful astringent, contracted [the human] soul to the very small dimensions of selfishness; and God was forsaken, and fellow-creatures forsaken, and man retired within himself, and became totally governed by narrow and selfish principles and feelings."[7] It is difficult to avoid the conclusion that we have become morally shrunken and shriveled in relation to other creatures. Foolishly, we think that God, or the "joy-giving Power," is only interested in the human species. We suffer from the spiritual impoverishment of thinking that animals are just here for us—for our own selfish purposes, and that our proper mission is simply to serve ourselves, or our own species.

At its best, religion can help us break free, to see further than ourselves, further than our own wants. It can help us reconnect with the world of creatures, to celebrate them, to reverence their life, to feel their pain, and to be active in their service. That, at least, is the promise of religion.

But there is also a case against religious belief. Far from liberating us from what Evans calls "sectarianism, tribalism and fundamentalism," it can enslave us even further to them, and to one other "ism" especially, namely "humanism." By "humanism" I mean here the ideology summed up in that great Protagorean maxim that "man is the measure of all things." When that happens, purely human wants, needs, and satisfactions are viewed as the goal of all created beings. And when cast in a religious form, "humanism" can frustrate, restrict, even stunt our moral growth. Nowhere, sadly, is this clearer than in our treatment of the animal world.

Instead of helping us to celebrate other creatures, religious leaders often speak as if animals were not there at all—as if we were the only species that mattered, and as if all creation was just theater or background to the real world of us human beings. Far from helping people to see animals as fellow creatures, to enjoy them (in the proper sense of the word), to marvel at them, and appreciate the beauty and complexity of their world, so often religious people are precisely those people who have not seen, have not appreciated, have not celebrated, and therefore have little to offer. So often religious people think, and behave, and worship, as if the world of animals were invisible.

Even more: far from helping people deepen their sense of reverence for all living beings, so often religious thinkers devise intellectual means of limiting that sense of reverence as if it were somehow childish or irrational, like an embarrassing habit we should grow out of. Instead of celebrating the kinship of all life, theologians devise even more ingenious ways of distinguishing ourselves from animals, as if evolutionary biology never existed. And even when someone speaks up for the animals, they seldom manage more than the usual "humans come first," which (decoded) more often than not means "only humans really matter."

The irony is that while the issue of animals is for many religious people a small, even marginal issue, it is—in terms of suffering alone—one of the major moral issues of our day. There is now ample evidence in peer-reviewed scientific journals that all mammals at least experience not just physical pain but also mental suffering, including terror, stress, fear, anxiety, trauma, anticipation, and foreboding, and that only to a lesser or greater degree than we do ourselves. Once this is grasped, it becomes apparent that we live in a much more sensitive and fragile world than many have supposed, and our duty of care is correspondingly greater.

But when it comes to compassion for animals, where are the religious voices? In the European Treaty of Amsterdam (which came into force in 1999), Member States agreed to recognize the status of animals as sentient beings, rather than as simply agricultural commodities. It asked Member States to "pay full regard to the welfare requirements of animals." But then the Treaty goes on to stipulate that States should do this "while respecting the legislative or administrative provisions and customs of the Member States relating to religious rites. . . ."[8] In other words, religion has become in European law a ground for *not* respecting the welfare of animals. What does that say about us, about our traditions, about our religion?

In addition, hardly a week goes by without concern for animals being ridiculed in the press, and by the religious press in particular. The most recent example is from *Zenit*, the international Catholic news agency, which ridiculed religious concern for companion animals. It singled out religious rites for animals as examples of imbalance, even "shades of *Animal Farm*." And what are these practices? Among others, what it disparagingly, if amusingly, calls "bark mitzvahs," as well as "pet funerals," and "pet-friendly worship services."[9] Of course there can be over-indulgence of companion animals, as there can be of human companions, but it is wrong to sneer at religious celebrations of human–animal relationships. Many who keep animals develop a close spiritual bond with their companions, and a religious "last rite" that gives thanks for the life of the animal concerned and commends it into the hands of God is, in Christian terms at least, wholly justifiable. "To those suffering such bereavement, it is as inconceivable that the body of their departed companion should be thrown out as garbage without a prayer as it would be in the case of the dead body of any human companion."[10]

Also noteworthy is the attempt by hunting supporters to set themselves up as a "religion" to stop the British Government from legislating against hunting with dogs. The creation of nothing less than a "Free Church of Country Sports" is envisaged. One supporter was reported to have said: "There are so many parallels between country sports and established religions: we also have regalias, we have our own language and our own art. Those in the Jewish faith blow a horn, the *shofar*, and so do we. Hunting is a form of ritualised killing—in our case the odds of actual killing are stacked in favor of the animal to escape." He goes on: "We baptise children by blooding them of the blood of that which we kill. Is this any more strange than dressing them in white and totally submerging them in water?"[11]

I know of no religion, and no sacred scripture, that justifies the infliction of suffering on wild animals for the sake of sport. Religious communities need to search themselves, examine their consciences, and ask why they have been so silent on this issue. My own Church, the Church of England—and I report this with the deepest shame—has virtually sold the pass. In an Open Letter to the Anglican Bishops before the final debate in the House of Lords, I tried to spell out the theological and moral considerations that had been overlooked in the debate. (The letter is reproduced as an Appendix at the end of this book.) All, sadly, to no avail. No fewer than ten bishops, including Oxford, Chelmsford, Bath and Wells, Guildford, Hereford, Peterborough, Salisbury, St. Albans, Portsmouth, and one former Archbishop in the House of Lords, spoke or voted in favor of the continuance of hunting.[12]

Martin Buber famously said that, "Nothing so hides the face of God as religion." We must face up to the fact that our religious traditions—the same traditions that hold out so much hope to humankind—are often the means by which human beings sustain their self-interest. My conviction is that no religion that leads us to insensitivity to suffering can be the real thing. In one sense, it really does not matter how we worship, what titles we may have, what garments we wear, or how we address the "mighty joy-giving Power" of which Younghusband wrote. What matters is that we do not become mean, selfish, heartless, unloving people; people who cannot see the suffering of others—animals or humans, people who cannot respond to their cries, or who have no imagination of what it is like for other creatures to live in misery. There is an ethical test of all religion, and it is this: does it make us live more loving, merciful, compassionate lives?

A few weeks ago, I received a communication from an anguished individual who objected that religious believers were often hypocrites. She wrote: "It makes me wonder what kind of god it is that these people worship—the god who is supposed to be upset if a sparrow falls? Of course, we all know that it has nothing to do with any gods. Just man, who regards animals as no different from a table or chair." And she concluded by saying that she was an atheist, and that "I have given up trying to understand mankind. I don't think there is any hope." This is a view that needs to be heard. Looked at in purely human terms, we may sympathize with the conclusion of the political philosopher William Godwin that the "whole history of the human species . . . appears a vast abortion."[13] It is difficult to examine impartially the immensity of the suffering we inflict upon animals worldwide in research, farming, and entertainment—to take only three examples—and to be sanguine about the moral sensibilities of human beings and their religion.

And yet it is precisely because—in purely human terms— the situation sometimes looks so hopeless, that we need the spiritual vision that only religion can, at its best, provide. Call it insight, revelation, illumination, mysticism, call it what you will, it alone can provide a ground for hoping, believing that we can do better—and most of all energizing us to do just that. It is only when we start having the courage to dream dreams that we find the moral energy to actually realize them. Where there is no vision, to adapt the line of the Psalmist, the animals (as well as humans) perish.

There is an urgent need for a much greater dialogue and understanding between religious believers and those working for animal protection. There are many thousands of animal-caring people working for humane goals who deserve, but do not often receive, support from religious authorities, even though the goals that they pursue are wholly consistent with mainstream religious teachings. It is time for religious traditions to meet the challenge of what is a growing worldwide movement of ethical sensitivity to animals. Animal protectionists have much to gain from an enlarged religious vision of the world, and, on closer inspection, many religious believers may be surprised to discover how much in their respective traditions supports a wider vision of peaceableness and compassion that explicitly includes animals.

2

Theology As If
Animals Mattered

This chapter outlines the challenges—ethical, theological, and spiritual—that animals pose to traditional Christian theology. It was originally published in Dialogue: A Journal of Religion and Philosophy *(Issue 26, April, 2006). The journal specializes in publishing material of relevance to those teaching high school students in Religious Studies and Philosophy, and I was especially grateful to have the opportunity to introduce some of the key ideas to a new generation of students.*

Animals, it must be admitted, have not figured prominently as an issue of theological or ethical concern within the Christian tradition. If anything, the issue has been a non-issue for Christians, who have relegated animals to the margins of theological enquiry. Yet ethical sensitivity to animals has grown massively during the last thirty years, and, undoubtedly, the ideas of the movement have been making steep inroads into conventional thinking about the place of humans—as well as animals—in creation. Philosophers have led the way in advancing what has been termed "a new ethic" for our treatment of animals.

Christian theology, however, has been slow to respond to this new sensitivity. Even now, many theologians refuse to consider the topic, regarding it as one of "emotionalism" and "sentimentality." In fact, they could not be more wrong. Concern for animals, as many philosophers have shown, has a strong rational basis. As Andrew Rowan has commented, during the last thirty years, moral philosophers have written more on the topic of human responsibility to other animals than their predecessors wrote during the previous three thousand years.

Someone recently remarked to me that the animal issue is for Christians "at a stage somewhat similar to the feminist issue forty years ago." Back then, many Christians were openly scornful of feminism and women's rights (some still are of course); but, in fact, feminist thought has challenged Christian thinking about the status of women, and Christianity has made significant changes as a consequence. The traditional Christian view that women should be subordinate to men is seldom articulated—at least in that crass form—today.

I want here to briefly sketch some of the challenges that the animal issue raises for traditional Christian thinking. My own view is that, although theologians scarcely realize it, there are powerful challenges—ethical, theological, and spiritual—that have yet to be heeded, let alone fully wrestled with.

Ethical Challenges: Beyond Gastrocentricity

Firstly, the ethical challenge. For all of its history, Christianity has been overwhelmingly concerned ethically with human beings—their life, status, and welfare. Animals have occasionally had a look in—as demonstrated, for example, by the chapter on animal pain in C. S. Lewis's *The Problem of Pain*—but mostly Christian ethicists have simply ignored animals. The lives of animals and their suffering have hardly registered as a blip on the theological radar. Far from seeing this as myopic or a weakness, most theologians have championed anthropocentricity. "The Word of God is concerned with God and man," maintains Karl Barth,[1] which of course inevitably makes animals a "marginal" problem in ethics.[2] Theology becomes little more than anthropology.

This idea has been buttressed by another, even more pervasive idea, namely that animals are put here for our use. It is summed up in a question put to me by one of my students at Oxford. "I found your lecture very interesting, Dr. Linzey, but there is one thing I don't understand: what are animals for—if they are not to be eaten?" The question was sincerely meant,

but indicates how unthinkingly anthropocentric, even gastro-
centric, Christian thought has become. The purpose or *telos*
of animals is assumed to be identical with human needs.

Of course, the notion that animals are here for our use
cannot be claimed to be a specifically Christian idea. It originated with Aristotle, if not before. "Since Nature makes nothing without some end in view, nothing to no purpose, it must
be that nature has made them [animals and plants] for the
sake of man" wrote Aristotle.[3] The idea was taken over by
St. Thomas Aquinas who gave it a theological gloss: it was
by divine providence that non-rational beings should serve
the higher species: "Hence it is not wrong for man to make
use of them [animals] either by killing or in any other way
whatever."[4] Almost all the classical exponents of the Christian
tradition, including Reformed theologians like Martin Luther
and John Calvin, have concurred. And in case it is thought
that Thomism has run its course, even the *Catholic Catechism*
of 1994 restates the essentials: "God willed creation as a gift
addressed to man," and again: "Animals, like plants and inanimate beings, are by nature destined *for the common good of
past, present and future humanity.*"[5]

One needs to step back a little in order to grasp the astonishing nature of the claims being made. We have become so
familiar with them that their sheer extraordinariness is often
overlooked. Is it obvious that the Creator who creates and sustains million of species only cares for one of them? Is it really
credible that throughout the long period of the evolution of life
on this planet that all species have no other *telos*—save that of
serving humankind? And, more incredible still, have they no
other function, save that of filling our stomachs—even, one
might add, those thousands of species we cannot eat due to
their inedibility? If God's will is that humans should eat all species, it is remarkable how few can actually be eaten without
gastronomic disturbance. And what of those millions of years of
evolution when there were no humans for animals to "serve"?

Once one begins to take on board such questions (and
many others I could mention), it becomes clear that Christian
ethics have become the prisoner of a range of assumptions
that badly need correction.

The problem becomes even more acute when one considers that the biblical material offers a range of positive views of animals. It is often supposed that the Bible supports a human "supremacist" view of animals, and specifically endorses the notion that animals are put here for human use. In fact, the first is only biblical in a highly qualified way, and the second is not biblical at all. The Bible nowhere says that animals are simply made for human betterment and that we can do what we like without moral limits. There are notions of kindness, responsibility, even communion, with animals in many books of the Bible. We do not have to look far. God's covenant is expressly made with all living creatures (Genesis 9:9–11). Sabbath peace is the goal of all creation (Genesis 2:1–3). God's "tender mercies are over all his works" (Psalm 145:9). It is a righteous person who "regards the life of his beast" whereas the unrighteous are "cruel" (Proverbs 12:10). The Book of Job even compares humans unfavorably with the Leviathan and the Behemoth (Chapters 40–41). Almost every Christian knows that God has given humans "dominion" over animals (Genesis 1:28), but hardly any seem to know that in the following verse God decrees a vegetarian diet (v. 29).

Of course, not all the verses in the Bible unambiguously support a pro-animal position. The Bible was written by human beings and principally focusses on the narratives of God's dealings with humans. Not everything in the Bible supports compassion and kindness for either humans or animals. There is, as Gerd Lüdemann reminds us, "the unholy" in Holy Scripture—neither human nor animal rights can be read simplistically from its pages.[6] Nevertheless, a Christian ethic that had attended thoughtfully to the positive voices that are there in scripture would not have countenanced the kind of unremitting exploitation of animals that we witness today.

Theological Challenges: Seeing with Different Eyes

Secondly, theological challenges. As we have noted, for most of its history the Christian tradition has not thought that God cares much—if at all—for other creatures. The result is unsurprising: Christians have not cared much either.

There is a long history of terrible dicta by theologians indicating indifference to animal suffering. The Jesuit Joseph Rickaby is by no means the worst:

> Brute beasts, not having understanding and therefore not being persons, cannot have any rights. . . . We have no duties of charity, nor duties of any kind, to the lower animals, as neither to stocks and stones.7

The placing of duties to animals here in the same category as our (non)duties to plants and inanimate objects is revealing to say the least. What it reveals especially is the low or nonexistent value accorded to animals in (this version of) Catholic theology. We can only presume that we owe nothing to animals because their Creator cares nothing for them. But how likely is it that a God who creates millions, if not billions, of species only cares for one of them? Of course, God may not care for all species equally, but why would the Creator want to give life to beings whose welfare is a matter of total indifference?

Once the biblical insight is grasped that God really does care for all creatures, we are forced to grapple with an other-than-anthropocentric view of the world. What value (or use) other creatures may have to us is an entirely different issue from their value to Almighty God. We cannot assume (as does so much historical and contemporary theology) that what is of benefit to us is automatically God's will. Our own estimations of our own needs and welfare cannot be the only basis for determining our relations with fellow creatures. Christian theology in that regard seems to have baptized an essentially utilitarian view of other-than-human creatures. No, that phrase "other-than-human" should stand. It is remarkably difficult to find non-pejorative language for animals and this is my little attempt. Only rarely have theologians had the imagination to grasp with James M. Gustafson that "the *theos* is not the guarantor of human benefits. . . . The chief end of God may not be the salvation of man."8

Poets, like Christina Rossetti, have penetrated further than most theologians:

> And other eyes than ours
> Were made to look on flowers. . . .
> The tiniest living thing
> That soars on feathered wing,
> Or crawls among the long grass out of sight
> Has just as good a right
> To its apportioned portion of delight
> As any King.[9]

We who envisage ourselves as the kings of creation have failed to see that God has created a multi-eyed universe. Ours are not the only eyes through which God looks out on the world. Through the Holy Spirit, the giver of life and inspirer of all, God experiences the creation as it were *from the inside*, and sees and feels through all the creatures of the earth.

Having grasped the other-than-human interests of the Creator, we shall be able to perceive central doctrines like incarnation and redemption with new eyes. As I suggest in *Animal Theology*, incarnation needs to be seen—not as the Yes of God to human flesh (still less just to male flesh) but to *all* flesh. The incarnation is God's love affair with all fleshly creatures. The idea may sound new but was, in fact, anticipated by Patristic writers. St. Athanasius, for example, writes of the Logos producing "a single melody":

> Extend[ing] his power everywhere, illuminating all things, visible and invisible, containing and enclosing them in himself, [giving] life and everything, everywhere, to each individually and to all together creating an exquisite single euphonious harmony.10

As well as re-visioning the incarnation as cosmic in significance, so we need to envisage redemption as truly inclusive. We are not souls to be plucked out of an alien matter at the end of time, rather we are one part of a drama of redemption that involves all creation. The Logos is the origin and destiny of all created things. Theology has hardly begun to articulate basic Christian convictions in the light of its doctrine of creation. How can the acts of incarnation and redemption be *smaller* than creation itself? Our wholly human-regarding God is too small to be credible.

There is another reason why theology should embark upon this course as a matter of urgency. Ludwig Feuerbach famously argued that Christianity is nothing other than the self-aggrandizement, even the deification of the human species.[11] To avoid this charge, theology needs to show how it can provide what it promises—namely a truly Godward (rather than a simply anthropocentric) view of the world. Its obsession with human beings to the exclusion of all else betokens a deeply unbalanced doctrine of God the Creator. Animal theology can help save Christians from the idolatry of self-worship.

One further point should be emphasized. We may recall that Aquinas regarded animals as non-rational, and that idea has in turn influenced centuries of Christian thought. But, without immodesty, we know more about animals today than did St. Thomas. There is now emerging evidence that mammals (at least) are self-aware and have the rudiments (at least) of rationality, defined as the ability to direct action to certain preconceived goals. There is, in addition, considerable evidence of sentiency, including fear, stress, anxiety, foreboding, anticipation, and terror.

Once the empirical evidence concerning animal self-awareness and sentiency is taken into account, the issue of theodicy becomes much more troubling than previous theologians have admitted. Brian Horne, like many "science and religion" and ecotheologians, suggests that "Modern zoology leads us to believe that death and sickness, earthquakes and floods, have always been part of the structure of the planet. . . ." And that such a perspective "require[s] us to view pain and death not as evil and outrageous, arising out of some act in the distant past but as plain and inescapable facts of biological existence." The result is that we should learn to regard these "occasions" in both the human and animal sphere as "occasions for love," so that the worst that evil could do to such love "would be to provide it with fresh opportunities for loving."

But, as I respond elsewhere:

We may fail to recognize the face of Christ in a theory of a world created by God in which hundreds, thousands, even millions of years of sickness and death are experienced by animal creatures, and latterly by human creatures, simply to facilitate "fresh opportunities for loving." What can we conclude about a kind of love which wants to perpetuate opportunities for itself, the whole possibility of which is itself predicated on the existence of a created world of gross unloveliness?12

Theologians have hardly begun to wrestle with the implications of animal sentiency for a decent theodicy. The idea that divine justice can be vindicated in the face of the vast suffering of evolution by simply proposing one species' capacity for love is a sign of how far we have to go in grasping the enormity of the problem.

Spiritual Challenges: Re-learning that We Are Not God

Thirdly, the spiritual challenges. Whenever concerns about animals are raised in a theological context, it is not long before the retort is heard: "But we are made in the image of God." That phrase is used as a trump to stop all further argument. But it is worth pondering what kind of "trump" it really is. In its original context in Genesis Chapter 1, humans are made in the image of God (v. 26), given dominion (v. 28), and then prescribed a vegetarian diet (v .29). The granting of the image is inextricably related to the exercise of dominion and the maintaining of God's peace in creation. We interpret dominion as little short of despotism, but understood in context, the image and dominion mean that we are entrusted to exercise power in a god-like way and in accordance with God's moral will. Image and dominion are integral to the commission to care for the world that God has made. Far from being a justification of wanton treatment, our power *can only be justified* in so far as it reflects and embodies divine will. And since the God in whose image we are made is holy, loving, and just, then our dominion can only be likewise.

But we must go further, and make one vital link in interpretation. Understood Christologically—that is, in terms of the person of Jesus Christ—power can never be its own justification. The power of God in Jesus is expressed in *katabasis*, humility, sacrificial loving, suffering with and for those who are oppressed. In short: the lordship of Christ *means* service. Seen from this perspective, human dominion over animals can never be a cost-free ride. As I have summarized elsewhere: "The old view is expressed by Keith Ward in his paraphrase of Genesis 1. He argues that 'man' is a made a 'god' in creation and that creatures should 'serve him.' The new view should be significantly different: given our God-given power and lordship over creation, it is *we* who should *serve creation*. The inner logic of Christ's lordship is the sacrifice of the higher for the lower; not the reverse. If the humility of God in Christ is costly and essential, why should ours be less so?"[13]

Questions will inevitably be raised about the Gadarene swine, Jesus' apparent fish-eating, and Peter's vision in Acts. There is no simple way of answering all the problems that arise from the biblical accounts, still less of harmonizing them. But, no matter the details, we can be clear about the contours. What Jesus offers us is a paradigm of inclusive moral generosity that extends to the poor, the disadvantaged, and the outcast. If we take that model as our inspiration, then it is possible to construct an authentically Jesus-shaped ethic of generosity that extends to the "least of all" in our day, including all suffering creatures.

The claim of animal theology is that humans will find themselves a freer species when they let go of previous notions of god-like supremacy over other creatures, and instead see themselves as the servant species commissioned by God. Freer in this one respect especially: the desire to control. Power enslaves the powerful as much as the victim. Freed of the Protagorean maxim that we are "the measure of all things," and that all species are here for our benefit, we shall be able to exercise the spiritual discipline of "letting be."

Of course, we need an active service toward other creatures, which involves curtailing our own greed and limiting our abuse, nothing less than a program of progressive disengagement from injury to animals. But first and foremost, we need to find the time to contemplate other living things as fellow creatures of the same God. The challenge is to find the means of discovering their value in the sight of God, and of celebrating their lives. So much exploitation and wantonness stems from a kind of spiritual blindness in which we fail to see their God-given value.

That is why I have risked ridicule and written a book of liturgical resources called *Animal Rites: Liturgies of Animal Care*. Its purpose is to help Christians "hear the divine rejoicing throughout the whole earth":

> Help us to wonder, Lord
> to stand in awe;
> to stand and stare;
> and so to praise you for the richness of the world
> you have laid before us.
> Christ in all things
> restore our senses,
> and give us again
> that experience of joy
> in all created things.[14]

Rational argument is, of course, important, and has its uses. But reason has to begin somewhere. More precisely, it has to begin with something *given*. In the words of Charles Péguy: "Everything begins in mysticism and ends in politics."[15]

At the heart of the new—now increasingly worldwide—sensitivity to animals is a fundamental change of perception. That change can be described quite simply. It is a move away from the idea that animals are things, machines, tools, commodities, here for our use, or means-to-human-ends, to the idea that animals as God-given sentient beings have their own intrinsic value, dignity, and rights. This is basically a spiritual insight, nothing less than a discovery of what is integral to the confession of God as Creator.

If the issue of animals arouses passion and debate, it is because what is at stake is the true status of animals as fellow-creatures with us in God's world. Animal theology stands or falls by this most basic insight: that animals are worth something in themselves because they are valued by God. This is a moral and spiritual discovery, as objective and as important as any other fundamental discovery, whether it be of stars or planets, of the existence of atoms, or some aspect of the human psyche. In years to come, we may be astonished that it took us so long to learn so little.[16]

Animal Rights
and AnimalTheology

*This essay situates the notion of animal rights in contemporary
debate and responds to some of the media caricatures of the animal movement. What is lacking in most popular commentary
is an appreciation of the history of philosophical thought about
animals, and a recognition that the notion of "animal rights"
builds upon previous "humanitarian" traditions. Although the
movement cannot be classed as "religious" per se, I try to show
how rights theory resonates with insights from Christian theology. The essay is a revised version of the Preface to the collection I edited with Paul Barry Clarke, titled* Animal Rights: A
Historical Anthology, *published by Columbia University Press
in 2005.*

The concept of "animal rights," and the movement that has
grown up around it, have been the subject of vigorous commentary, some enthusiastic, others much less so. "The animal
rights movement is pagan," maintains one recent commentator. "Greenery," we are told, "puts man, whose nature God
takes to himself in Christ Jesus, Mary's son, below the level
of the animals (or, in Greenspeak, the non-human animals)."
"It is not accidental that a characteristic of Greenery is that
its practitioners denigrate, and even hate, mankind," we are
assured. "Theirs is a world in which man is deracinated and
nature deified."[1]

Charges of this kind are increasingly common in the popular media, but these are from an Oxford academic (formerly
Principal of Plater College) and a well-known translator of

papal texts. That the concept of animal rights should be controversial is hardly surprising; that the movement should also be subject to criticism is only appropriate; but that an academic should feel free to use such intemperate language is symptomatic of the nature of current debate, or rather the lack of it.

In order to properly understand a given issue, one has to step back a little (sometimes a lot) and gain some perspective. That perspective can most readily be supplied by historical understanding—in this case of the long history of ethical discussion about the ethics of our treatment of animals. Among the more erroneous characterizations has been the portrayal of animal rights as little more than a post-1970s phenomenon, the tail end of "sixties" liberation movements that began (seriously) with civil rights and ended (ludicrously) with "furry creatures." The last and most implausible of all liberation movements, it is contended, that only illustrates the limitations, even ultimate illogicality, of liberation thinking. At a time when much "sixties" thinking has been revised or jettisoned, animal rights are thus commonly presented as the "one liberation too far"—and accordingly treated, even among the wise, with intellectual disdain.

And it must be admitted that advocates have themselves sometimes contributed to the view that animal rights are—in the most seductive word in the English language—"new." They have spoken all too readily of "new thought," "new ideas," "new paradigms," and "new ethics." Some of this may be justified—when, for example, outlining a novel campaign or policy development—but much of it contributes to the widespread perception that moral thinking about animals represents a contemporary bandwagon. Sometimes one fears that "animal advocates" (itself a not wholly enlightening, or endearing, term) have colluded in a caricature of themselves.

For a caricature it is. There is a long tradition of reflection on our ethical relations with animals—as far back as the Greeks, possibly earlier. Some of the world's most distinguished thinkers—including Plato, Aristotle, Augustine, Aquinas, Descartes, Hobbes, Locke, Schopenhauer, Nietzsche, and even Marx—have given time to the animals. That much of what they have said is now deemed unsatisfactory does not alter the fact that there is a rich tradition of thought of which we are (in more ways than one) inheritors. It is simply wrong to jettison this intellectual history, or to ignore it, as if we "post-moderns" had all the truth. Indeed, it is precisely because of the limitations of previous thought that we should engage it with renewed seriousness. We learn—or should—as much from our mistakes as from our achievements. And, of course, one person's limitation is another's creative opportunity.

It should be the task of educators to go beyond contemporary caricature and help students to grapple with the complex evolution of moral thought. History is invariably an antidote to superficiality. If the concept of animal rights deserves serious attention (as I believe it does), then educators have a duty to help students grapple with the historical provenance of the issue in question, and to understand why the ancients and pre-moderns thought differently from ourselves or, more truthfully, how (often without knowing it and with much less understanding) we simply reflect what they once uttered. Animal advocates, too, should more clearly embrace the fact that in previous ages, there were always some, albeit a minority, who took the trouble to register a moral problem in our treatment of animals.

Once this is grasped, we shall also be able to confront the misperception (often endorsed by advocates) that one or two books, or contemporary philosophers, have originated the idea of animal rights, or are the patriarchs of the movement, indeed the whole notion of a "movement"—conceived as a body of systematic ideas with a coherent strategy—is belied every time one reads activist literature with its diverse goals and perspectives. If there is a movement of ideas, it has had an altogether longer gestation, and has been furthered by a wide variety of poets, saints, philanthropists, and thinkers.

By rescuing moral concern for animals from the pens of just one or two contemporary philosophers, we do better justice to them (as honorable contributors to an ongoing moral tradition) and also to the cause of animals itself. No one person is *the* voice of animal rights—unless we are to be utterly myopic about the development of ideas—and for the sake of

the animals it is just as well, since the limitations of all thinkers become only too obvious over time. All thinkers about animals, even and especially contemporary ones, need a greater
humility in recognizing that their apparent success is only
a part of another's apparent failure. We are still a long way
off having an adequate or comprehensive conceptualization
of our moral obligations to animals. Premature attempts to
claim the philosopher's stone discourage fellow seekers, let
alone those who have yet to explore.

At the same time, there have been periods when sensitivity to animals reached decisive points of social embodiment.
The most obvious example is the attempts at organized animal
protection in the nineteenth century, which culminated in
the emergence of the English SPCA in 1824 and the American SPCA in 1866. What is now termed the "animal rights
movement" is more clearly indebted to that development than
anything else. Many now take for granted the gains in social
practice for which these organizations strove, but in fact they
were, in their time, moral feats of great daring. But they, in
turn, were dependent upon the work of moral thinkers before
them. In the same way, the organization of animal advocacy
in the twenty-first century is dependent upon a much broader
and deeper concern than post-1970s philosophy. Perhaps the
most skeptical philosopher of all, namely Nietzsche, could
write in 1874 that, "The deeper minds of all ages have had
pity for the animals, because they suffer from life and have
not the power to turn the sting of their suffering against themselves, and understand their being metaphysically." "The sight
of blind suffering is the spring of the deepest emotion," he
writes.[2]

That realization helps us to confront the third misperception of animal rights, namely that it is bolstered by anti-human
sentiment—misanthropy in revenge. There is no more common, or pernicious, claim than "those who love animals do so
because of their incapacity to love humans." (Why the corollary charge—that those who love humans are incapable of loving animals—is never articulated betokens partiality, however
understandable). Although it has been said (not without justification) that humans of all the species are the most unlov-

able, examination of the voices for animals throughout history does not support the charge of misanthropy. When one looks through the long list of diverse animal-concerned thinkers throughout the ages, one searches in vain to discover more than one or two misanthropes. Even the uncompromising Montaigne, writing in the sixteenth century, defends the just treatment of animals on the grounds that the unjust power we wield over them is the same that we exercise over other humans:

> On these terms we have our slaves. Were there not women in Syria called Climacides, who, crouching on all fours, served as footstools or step-ladders to enable the ladies to mount into their coaches? And the majority of free people, for a very slight consideration, surrender their life and being into the power of others. . . . We condemn everything that appears strange to us and which we do not understand; and we do the same in our judgment of the animals.3

Moreover, the charge cannot be sustained historically. Modern concern for animals can be traced back directly to the emergence of the "humanitarian movement"—as it has been called—of the nineteenth century. This movement expressly included slaves, children, and the poor, as well as animals, within its moral purview. The major figures of the animal protection movement in Britain—Lord Shaftesbury, William Wilberforce, and Fowell Buxton, to name only three—were distinguished by their concern for a wide range of animal and human causes. Indeed, Shaftesbury articulated his philosophy in deliberately inclusive terms: "I was convinced that God had called me to devote whatever advantages he might have bestowed upon me to the cause of the weak, the helpless, both man and beast, and those who had none to help them."4 The roots of organized animal advocacy do not lie in misanthropy, but in philanthropy.

At the same time, it cannot be denied that some animal advocates—a very tiny minority, frustrated by the pace of change—have indulged in anti-human polemic and even—most deplorable of all—allowed their emotions to be expressed through acts of violence. It goes without saying that these actions are unconscionable, and, most importantly of all, utterly inconsistent with the stated philosophy of animal-regarding thinkers throughout the ages. It is vital to see that violent animal rights people no more represent the cause of animals than football hooligans serve the sport of soccer. And we can know this by giving due consideration to the many voices that span more than three thousand years of (admittedly disparate, but nevertheless consistent) animal advocacy. It is not those who act violently to either animals or humans, but rather those who seek to live peaceably, who can properly claim to be a part of the movement for the ethical treatment of all sentient beings. Linguistically, "animal rights violence" is an oxymoron. Morally, it is self-contradictory. And historically, it is as inane as abolitionists who thought that they could better conditions for slaves by battering slavers.

Another misperception is that animal rights represent a form of "paganism" in which adherents jettison biblical insights and give themselves over not only to misanthropy but also to animal worship. The religious, specifically Christian, impulse to care for animals is nowhere better expressed than by Alexander Pope who maintains that humankind are "no less, in proportion, accountable for the ill use of their dominion over creatures of the lower rank of beings, than for the exercise of tyranny over their own species."[5] Although the religious have variously propounded a notion of God-given power over animals, they have at the same time pioneered a critique of the idea that power is its own self-justification. It is true that animal rights thinkers today are a rather diverse group that comprises both religious and anti-religious thinkers. There are some who believe that the whole notion of "God-given power" over animals is regressive, and others (like myself) who think it involves a special care for the weak and the vulnerable of all species. But it is folly to suppose that the whole movement is anti-religious or can be characterized as "secularized religion."

We know that because the founding figures of organized animal protection were themselves frequently religious and understood their mission as the embodiment of religious ideals. The founder of the 1824 English SPCA (as it then was), the Anglican priest Arthur Broome, conceived of the Society as a specifically Christian enterprise based on Christian principles. Neither is this an isolated example. The emergence of the modern, organized vegetarian movement both in America and Britain owes much to the founding support of the Bible-Christian Church that took seriously the divine injunction to be vegetarian (Genesis 1:29–30) and made vegetarianism compulsory among its members. Again, the movement for the abolition of vivisection enjoyed the active patronage of two esteemed Christians, Lord Shaftesbury and Cardinal Manning, and one historian even attributes the early success of the movement to "the religious tendency of the English nation" and "the warm sympathy of the clergy."[6]

Of course, organized religion has not always been so sympathetic to animal-friendly goals. There has been a negative tradition, represented principally by Augustine and Aquinas, which has excluded animals (more or less) from direct moral solicitude. But this tradition has gone through considerable development and is still in a process of change. The notion of animal rights has found modern champions, even in conservative Roman Catholic circles, as the following lines from Cardinal Heenan, former Archbishop of Westminster, indicate:

When I was young I often heard quoted a piece of Christian philosophy, which was taken as self-evidently true. It was the proposition that animals have no rights. This, of course, is true only in one sense. They are not human persons and therefore they have no rights, so to speak, in their own right. But they have very positive rights because they are God's creatures. If we have to speak with absolute accuracy we must say that God has the right to have all his creatures treated with respect.[7]

There is perhaps an even deeper connection between animal rights theorists and theology. Theorists commonly appeal to notions of "intrinsic value," "respect for sentient life," and often assume a deontological account of moral obligation that most naturally fits a religious, specifically theological, framework. Far from being a movement toward moral dissipation or relativity, many thinkers endorse, implicitly or explicitly, objective theories of moral obligation. From a theological perspective, I have argued, following Heenan, for the "*theos*-rights" of animals, based on God's prior right as Creator to have what is created treated with respect, and I have suggested that when "we speak of animal rights we conceptualise what is objectively owed to animals as a matter of justice by virtue of their Creator's right."[8]

But, it may be questioned, is the notion of "animal rights" a legitimate development of earlier conceptions of care and benevolence? And, moreover, are not the critics right that it represents a decisive rejection of earlier notions of rights based specifically on an appeal to "human" nature and dignity? Is Joseph Kirwan correct that "people who speak of 'rights' today generally mean something quite different from what philosophers of the last 2000 years have understood by *ius* [right] . . ." so that there "has been a shift in the concept of what it means to be human"?[9]

To answer the first question, we need to be aware that the movement for extending solicitude to animals has gone through various stages and has been shaped by different ideas—what I call the "humanitarian," "welfare," and "justice" conceptions of moral obligation. First came the simple "humanitarian" appeal to prevent cruelty and exercise kindness. This conceptualization resulted in the formation of the RSPCA and various humane organizations in the United States. Secondly, there was a more expansive notion of animal "welfare" that went beyond a simple focus on cruelty, and was concerned with suffering and well-being in the widest sense. And thirdly, there has been the inclusion of animals within the sphere of "justice"—of which the language of direct duties and rights has become the most obvious expression. Although these notions still overlap and jostle together (and it is by no means clear that one should wholly obliterate the others), it should be evident that there is a clear progression of ideas from one to the other. Very few theologians have suggested that our "dominion" is illimitable—and from that notion has gone (negatively) an expanding sense of what we have *no right* to do to animals, which has given rise (positively) to a deepening sense that animals have rights in themselves. Historically, the latter conceptualization has fed off the former. In other words: we are witnessing the development of a tradition of moral thought that culminates in the notion of "rights"—as the most contemporary expression of what is objectively owed to animals as a matter of justice—but that is built on previous notions of moral "limits" in relation to them.

To the second question, whether this development represents a different, wider conception of justice, the answer is plainly "yes." Animal rights thinkers use the concept of rights differently from most of their forebears, and want to include (usually all) sentient beings within their circle of moral obligation. To Kirwan, who argues that this somehow degrades specifically "human" rights or dignity, the answer has to be that there needs to be a better reason for rejecting the development of moral thought other than it is a development. The obvious parallel here is with the rights of children. For the same two thousand years—of which Kirwan speaks approvingly—there has also been a thoroughgoing rejection of the rights of children, and for many of the reasons cited against animals, specifically that children (at least infants) are incapable of acknowledging duties to us. In fact, according to animal rights theorists like myself, it is precisely the vulnerable and innocent status of sentient beings—such as infants and animals—that impels the granting of special moral solicitude.[10] And, as for humanity (actually adult humanity), our very "dignity" is enhanced—rather than diminished—by this active recognition.

Kirwan is right that our notion of "what it means to be human" has changed in this process, but is an odd notion of humanity that sees the extension of moral obligations as a threat to the "dignity" of the one species (as far as we know) capable of exercising them. It is difficult to see how "man is deracinated and nature deified" in a system of thought that places so much reliance upon human beings to act as the supreme moral agents. Far from "deracinating" humankind, in displaying a capacity for impartiality in weighing the moral claims of other sentient beings, we may connect with one of the deepest roots of our own nature, namely the desire for justice—and for all.

The Conflict between Ecotheology and Animal Theology

An invitation from Professor Roger Gottlieb to contribute to the Oxford Handbook of Religion and Ecology (Oxford and New York: Oxford University Press, 2006) provided me with an opportunity to explore the basic divergence of perspective between ecological and animal theology. Ecologists invariably look upon the system of predation as God-given and care more for "the whole" than they do for individual animals. Animal theologians, on the other hand, see "nature" as we now know it as incompatible with the good creation that God originally made. Nature is fallen and has a tragic quality; and individual sentients count—not just the system as a whole. What this means in practice is explored in relation to hunting for sport, vegetarianism, and conservation.

What do we see when we look at nature? As Max Weber famously said: "All knowledge comes from a point of view." What, then, are the points of view that make animal theology and ecological theology such apparently uncomfortable bedfellows? Of course, every reforming movement is notoriously hostile to those who "see" but do not yet "quite see" what *they* have seen, and so it is with animal and ecological theologies. On paper, the agreements appear so considerable that many cannot quite see that there *is* an issue of difference at all. Take, for example, some of the following "points of religious agreement in environmental ethics":

The natural world has value in itself and does not exist solely for human needs.

There is a significant continuity of being, between human and non-human living beings, even though human beings do have a distinctive role. This continuity can be felt and experienced.

Non-human living beings are morally significant, in the eyes of God and/or the cosmic order. They have their own unique relations to God, and their own places in the cosmic order.

Moral norms such as justice, compassion and reciprocity apply (in appropriate ways) both to humans and to non-human beings. The well-being of humans and the well-being of non-human beings are inseparably connected.[1]

No animal theologian would dissent from these key propositions, and so it appears that there is unanimity. But the world, and especially the world of nature, is not quite that straightforward. Animal theologians and ecological theologians still do not *see* the same things when they peer into "nature," or even if they see them, they "count" them in different ways.

Perhaps the best way of viewing the difference is to see through the eyes of Annie Dillard. Her *Pilgrim at Tinker Creek* is widely regarded as a testimony to ecological wisdom, and the author has been praised as "a writer of genuinely original vision to teach us anew 'To see a World in a grain of sand.'"[2] Dillard spends a year in the Roanoke Valley in the Blue Ridge Mountains of Virginia, a place called Tinker Creek. There, throughout the seasons of the year, she watches and waits. She encounters what may be one of the last remnants of a genuinely undisturbed ecosystem, at least for now. She observes and notes, and then philosophizes on the myriad of strange life forms that she encounters, and how they interrelate in ways that appear (to us) unaccountable and mysterious. But Dillard is not just a "nature writer," commonly understood as someone who wants to point out unusual or marvelous things, still less a "travel writer," who aims to bring new worlds to our attention; her underlying concern is to *make sense* of the world, or worlds, that lie around us. Her religious background, never specifically spelled out but always close to the surface, helps provide a kind of spiritual autobiography.

As the narrative moves on, the darkness of nature, as well as its delights, presses itself upon her. One form of life really does live at the expense of another. There is pain, apparent waste, futility, and premature destruction. The world that presages paradise becomes, on closer inspection, a hellish one. And she does not hide from our gaze the awfulness of what she discovers, but how is she meant to make sense of it?

The clues mount up. "It's chancy out there," we are told. "Dog whelks eat rock barnacles, worms invade their shells, shore ice razes them from the rocks and grinds them to a powder. Can you lay aphid eggs faster than chickadees can eat them? Can you find a caterpillar, can you beat the killing frost?"[3] "Evolution," it is suggested, "loves death more than it loves you or me."[4] Again, "We value the individual supremely, and nature values him not a whit." Perhaps she will have to extricate herself from the Creek in order to *remain* human, to prevent herself from becoming "utterly brutalized." And here the religious impulses to "make sense" become overwhelming:

> Either this world, my mother, is a monster, or I myself am a freak.
>
> Consider the former: the world is a monster. Any three-year-old can see how unsatisfactory and clumsy is this whole business of reproducing and dying by the millions. Yet we have not encountered any god who is as merciful as a man who flicks a beetle over on its feet. There is not a people in the world who behaves as badly as praying mantises. But wait, you say, there is no right and wrong in nature; right and wrong is a human concept. Precisely: we are moral creatures, then, in an amoral world. The universe that suckled us is a monster that does not care if we live or die—does not care if it itself grinds to a halt. It is fixed and blind, a robot programmed to kill. We are free and seeing; we can only try to outwit it at every turn to save our skins.[5]

Although her precise philosophy is difficult to discern, the various recognitions of parasitism force her to conclude that the universe is designed to be a self-sacrificing system. The references to priests and sacrifice increase. Can it really be that the Creator has so willed it to the advantage of humankind? "God *look* at what you've done to this creature [the sacrificial ram], look at the sorrow, the cruelty, the long damned waste!" she expostulates. "Can it possibly, ludicrously be for *this* that on this unconscious planet with my innocent kind I play softball all spring, to develop my throwing arm?"[6] Difficult though it is to summarize, the conclusion (at least) betokens resignation, even (paradoxically) "thanksgiving." As in Emerson's dream, she "ate the world":

> All of it. All of it intricate, speckled, gnawed, fringed, and free. Israel's priests offered the wave breast and the heave shoulder together, freely, in full knowledge, for thanksgiving. . . . And like Billy Bray [the nineteenth-century Methodist preacher— ed.] I go my way; and my left foot shouts "Glory," and my right foot says "Amen": in and out of Shadow Creek, upstream and down, exultant, in a daze, dancing, to the twin silver trumpets of praise.[7]

Time spent with Dillard is always rewarding because, excellent writer that she is, she helps us to see in an anguished and poetic way the currently fatalistic view of the world that is common among ecological theologians. She sees the pain, the waste, and the futility—according to Richard Adams, author of *Watership Down*, she is even "obsessed with Nature's apparently futile waste and indifference to suffering, to a degree no British writer (as far as I know) has been."[8] But the vital point to grasp is that there is no other world for which we should strive, no other world is morally or theologically available. We just have to bear it. The world is a self-murdering system of survival. Like Israel's priests we have to accept it and offer thanksgiving.

Ecological theologians reinforce Dillard's line almost to a tee, except that they usually go further. Not only is the world there to be eaten, it is manifestly God's will that it *should* be. I choose just three examples.

The first is from Richard Cartwright Austin, a prolific eco-theologian with more than four books to his credit, who extols the "beauty" of predation. In the context of a meditation on a fish eagle taking its prey, he writes:

> Now I think that death may be part of the goodness of God's creation, so long as death and life remain in balance with each. To eat, and finally to be eaten, are part of the blessing of God.9

The second is from the well-known exponent of creation theology, Matthew Fox, whose *Original Blessing*[10] did so much to encourage an alternative theological view of creation. In a conversation with Jonathon Porritt, he makes clear that he ascribes equal value to all parts of creation, but also endorses predation as God's will:

> One of the laws of the Universe is that we all eat and get eaten. In fact, I call this the Eucharistic law of the Universe, even Divinity gets eaten in this world. And so the key is not whether we are going to be doing some dying in the process of being here, but whether we kill reverently. And that, of course, means with gratitude. You know, in the Christian tradition, it's interesting that the sacrifice of Divinity is called eucharist, that is, "thank you," gratitude. Gratitude is, I think, the test of whether we are living reverently this dance of the equality of being on the one hand, but also the need to sacrifice and be sacrificed on the other.[11]

In both writers, killing, even of sentient creatures, is unambiguously God's will. We might even say that nature *is* God's will.[12] That is not just how the world *is*, but how it *should be*. The task is not to reject, or question such a world, or to be appalled by it, but to live reverently within it—with thanksgiving.

A third and similar, but rather more nuanced, view is provided by Jay B. McDaniel, another prolific writer on ecotheology. McDaniel has led the way in imaginatively combining "process theology" and ecological awareness. He sets his readers a poser drawn from the writings of that influential nature writer, Gary Snyder. The scenario takes place in the Chukchi Sea, just north of Western Alaska, where a friend of his had watched "with fascinated horror" as orcas methodically battered a grey whale to death. McDaniel asks us to envision God in relation to that spectacle. It is understandable, he notes, that we should feel empathy with the whale, and wonder why an all-powerful God could allow it to happen, but he suggests we ask a different question: "As the orca was chasing the grey whale in the Chukchi Sea, whose side was God on?" "The answer must be," writes McDaniel, that God was "on the side" of both creatures, 'to the exclusion of neither."[13] Since God wills the survival of both creatures, we must so envision God as immanent within both. From a process perspective, "things happen in the universe which God does not will, but which are nevertheless part of God's life." Process thinkers, says McDaniel, may discern a "fallen" dimension in predator–prey relations, "but they also see God as partly responsible for their existence in the first place." In short, the "fall" into carnivorous existence was lured by God, with co-operation from creatures. It was a "fall upward."[14]

It should be clear that whatever the individual sentiments of the writers we have considered (and McDaniel, for one, has been in the forefront of encouraging Christian concern for animals), it is difficult to see how their perspectives can provide a robust theological case against the human killing of other sentient creatures. In the end, not just death, but killing is wholly or partly God's will. Again, that is not just how the world *is*, it is how it *should be*. We have to resign ourselves to it. What "counts" is the "system," "nature as a whole," "creation as God made it," individual creatures are just pawns in the game or, rather, means to another's end. There is no "dilemma" save that provided by our own, misguided, moral senses.

Now, I do not want to underplay the significance of what may be termed the "realist" perception of nature that these writers, variously, express. Indeed, ironically, thanks to "ecological awareness" such a perception of nature is now widespread. Nature films on television have vastly reinforced it by regularly focusing on nature as an untrammeled struggle for survival. Every schoolboy or schoolgirl now knows that it is a "jungle" out there, where human notions of right and wrong really do not apply—at least to individuals. Animal protectionists, like me, are accused of simply not facing up to the world as it is.[15]

But I do want to challenge the notion that this perception is the *only* one that the study of nature can afford us, and that it can be sustained solo without obscuring other insights arguably much more fundamental, one in particular. So, let me return to my starting point: what do we see when we look at nature? The rival perception bequeathed by historic theology is to see nature not "as a whole," but rather as "un-whole," as tragic, incomplete, divided against itself, even "fallen." Such a perception does not deny pain, suffering, and apparent waste and futility in nature, rather it begins with it, and seeks to relate it to the wider Christian themes of creation and redemption. St. Paul classically gives this expression when he writes of the creation in bondage, suffering in travail, awaiting its deliverance by the redeemed children of God (Romans 8:14–24).

This idea has found wide resonance within Western culture. Even Nietzsche, surely one of the most unromantic of thinkers as well as one who resolutely resists theologizing of any kind, writes—as we have seen—of how the "sight of blind suffering is the spring of the deepest emotion" and how animals cannot "understand their being metaphysically.[16] That is why Nietzsche goes on to postulate that nature needs human interpreters, specifically "the artist," "the philosopher," and also, most revealingly, "the saint":

> In him [the saint] the ego is melted away, and the suffering of his life is, practically, no longer felt as individual, but as the spring of the deepest sympathy and intimacy with all living creatures: he sees the wonderful transformation scene that the comedy of "becoming" never reaches, the attainment, at length, of the high state of man after which all nature is striving, that she may be delivered from herself.[17]

Although he would scarce have wanted it described this way, Nietzsche is here articulating the fundamental Christian hope for creation's redemption. From this perspective what is significant about creation is not what it currently is but what it can become by grace. What is most telling is that we can hear the sighs and groans of inarticulate (to us) fellow creatures. Martin Luther, in his commentary on Romans 8, says that "anyone who searches into the essences and the functioning of the creatures rather than into their sighings and earnest expectations is certainly foolish and blind" because "he does not know that also the creatures are created for an end."[18]

Although it is largely unrepresented in modern theology, theologian Paul Tillich well grasped the point in his sermon "Nature also mourns for a lost good," inspired by Schelling's poignant line: "A veil of sadness is spread over all nature, a deep unappeasable melancholy over all life," a sadness "manifest through the traces of suffering in the face of all nature, especially in the faces of animals."[19] The upshot is that nature "is not only glorious; it is also tragic. It is suffering and sighing with us. No one who has ever listened to the sounds of nature with sympathy can forget their tragic melodies."[20] But because the tragedy of nature is bound to the tragedy of human beings, we can hope that, as humans are redeemed by grace, there is also hope for nature itself. Significantly, the Eucharist, far from being a legitimization of predation, as Fox supposes, becomes a symbol for Tillich of what E. L. Mascall once called the "Christification"[21] of nature itself: "Bread and wine, water and light, and all the great elements of nature become the bearers of spiritual meaning and saving power."[22]

The result, then, of attending to this other perception is to affirm the ambiguity of creaturely existence. Creation is good, even "very good," yet it is also incomplete and unfinished. We perceive a symmetry in nature, but one that points beyond itself. As Karl Barth says: there is both a "yes" and a "no" in creation. A "yes" because God loves it, and values it, and creates it for an eternal relationship with the Divine. But there is also a "no" because it is not divine, and like all earthly stuff, it is in its own way tragically incomplete without divine grace.[23] More poignantly still, Albert Schweitzer speaks of creation as the "ghastly drama of the will-to-live divided against itself."[24]

Ecotheologians commonly resist this conclusion, and maintain that seeing nature as less than what it should be devalues God's gift of creation. What we need, they say, is a robust acceptance that all nature is *unambiguously* good as it is (it should follow of course that the same should be said of human nature—but that logical step is never taken), even that it is "sacred." In the blunt words of Anne Primavesi: "If Nature is seen as 'not God,' then this licenses human control over it."[25] But this is a *non sequitur*; deifying all nature does not by itself save it from exploitation. On the contrary, one of the weaknesses of McDaniel's approach, based on process theology, is that God is eclipsed in the most vital work of all, namely redemption. For how can God, logically, redeem himself or herself? The attempt to "sacralize" nature is understandable as a protest against ruthless exploitation, but as a theological position it simply undercuts the whole human-responsibility-for-ecology program. The bottom line is that the transcendence of God constitutes the hope of a *this-worldly* redemption. A God that is so compromised by immanence that he or she cannot escape the eternal earthly round is not one that can offer redemption for any creature, let alone command "responsible stewardship."

It is now appropriate to consider the divergent practical implications that flow from these different perspectives. Some words of caution are required. Not all ecologists are anti-animals and vice versa. One of the remarkable things about Dillard's work is that, although she seemingly resolves the dilemma through resignation, she is also acutely conscious of the pains that animals have to undergo. So it is with at least some ecologists, and it should be noted that some animal advocates are often at the forefront of ecological campaigns. Nevertheless, there is typically a divide when it comes to practical issues, which is often acutely felt by those who campaign in these areas. I select just three.

The first relates to the ethics of killing, and vegetarianism in particular. If God wills a self-sacrificing system of survival, as many ecotheologians suppose, then there cannot be any theological basis for desisting from killing, not just plants, but also sentient animals (humans, too, if one is to be strictly logical). This is why so many ecotheologians are not vegetarians or, if they are, why they appeal not to straightforward ethical considerations about killing, but to environmental factors, like the harmful effects of intensive farming, and the deforestation commonly involved in rearing cattle in the developing world. Although some ecotheologians will adopt vegetarianism on these grounds, or because of the "unnatural methods" of factory farming, on the general issue of killing, they will most likely be found on the side of those who do not see a "moral" issue at all.[26]

Animal theologians, on the other hand, see vegetarianism as the first step toward the creation of a violence-free world, and even though absolute consistency is hard to embody, they will recommend it as a symbolic and practical renunciation. In the trenchant words of Stephen R. L. Clark: "Honourable men may honourably disagree about some details of human treatment of the non-human, but vegetarianism is now as necessary a pledge of moral devotion as was the refusal of emperor-worship in the early Church. . . . Those who still eat flesh when they could do otherwise have no claim to be serious moralists."[27]

It is important to make explicit the *theological* basis of this divergence. For animal theologians, the issue of not killing except when essential is not just about ethical precepts. It is about a contrasting vision of what humans should be in creation. Animal theologians take seriously the idea that humans are made in God's image—in the image of a just, holy, and loving God—and therefore expect humans to acknowledge duties to animals who cannot acknowledge them in return. *Human* killing in creation is attended (in most cases) by free will and moral choice. Therefore, animal killing cannot provide a basis for justifying human acts. As the writer and theologian C. S. Lewis rightly observed: "It is our business to live by our own law not by hers [Nature's]."[28] Moreover, theological vegetarianism has an anticipatory character: "By refusing to kill and eat meat, we are witnessing to a higher order of existence, implicit in the Logos, which is struggling to be born in us. By refusing to go the way of our 'natural nature' or our 'psychological nature,' by standing against the order of unredeemed nature we become signs of the order of existence for which all creatures long."[29]

The second concerns suffering. One might think that, even if animal and ecotheologians were divided about killing, at least they would be united in opposing the infliction of suffering on animals, but not so. Greenpeace and other environmental organizations do not campaign against hunting for sport, or even trapping for fur. The great campaigns on these issues have been waged not with the tacit support of ecologists but rather in the face of their opposition. In England, even "green" bishops, like Hugh Montefiore, John Oliver, and Jim Thompson, have lined up in favor of the continuance of fox and deer hunting. The appeal is invariably not to justice for individual sentients, or the undesirability of humans obtaining pleasure from chasing and killing animals, but rather to general environmental considerations, and most especially to predation in nature. Foxes, we are told, are not "kindly in their ways" and "nature is not a kindly place." Bishop Thompson opined that those "who believe in God must come to terms with a creation of mutual hunting and eating," as if nature were a moral textbook or capable of relieving us of our obligations as moral agents.[30] Even worse was the pronouncement of a former Archbishop of York that hunting with dogs could be justified because of the "fascination" which people have with "the kind of competitive encounter that one has with a wild animal."[31]

Again, it is important to grasp that the issue is not just about morality. If one begins with the perception of the tragic character of nature as locked in, even against itself, to bondage, then intensifying that bondage by exploiting the natural antipathy that one creature has for another is a sub-Christian pursuit. As the former Dean of Westminster, Edward Carpenter, argued, hunting is "in the strictest sense of the word, deplorable . . . it is to fall back into that bondage, into that predatory system of nature, from which the Christian hope has always been that not only man but the whole natural order itself is to be released and redeemed." Hunting does "violence to Christian faith and witness[es] to a lower order than that redeemed creation to which Christ leads us."[32]

The third concerns human "management" of the environment, and animals in particular. One might think given the high doctrine of creation as God's will that ecologists would be content to "let it be" according to its own perceived God-given law. On the contrary, ecologists typically espouse an *active* form of management, bolstered by the notion of "dominion," in which humans have a right and a duty to intervene. If this management were confined to helping ailing species or individuals within species, then animal theologians could only applaud, but "conservationists" go much further. In the interest of the "whole" (for they often claim to know what the interest of the whole is), they appear only too eager to sacrifice one species for another, even if this means ruthless and indiscriminate killing and the infliction of considerable suffering. I give two examples drawn from the United Kingdom.

The first is the case of the ruddy duck. First brought to Britain in the 1940s for ornamental purposes, some escaped and bred in the wild. Their numbers increased and there is now a population of around five thousand in Britain. The British Government is currently planning their systematic eradication. The putative justification for this killing ("culling" is the word used by conservationists) is that the ruddy mates with another non-native species called the white-headed duck, and hybridization occurs. As a contracting party to the Convention on Biological Diversity (CBD), the British Government is required to control or eliminate "alien" species that "threaten ecosystems, habitats or species."[33] The upshot is that around a thousand ruddies have already been killed (mainly through shooting) and another four thousand killings are planned. In the words of the Department for Environment, Food and Rural Affairs (DEFRA), the "ruddy duck control trial final report (2002) concluded that there is an 80% certainty that the population can be reduced to fewer than 175 birds in between four and six years, at a cost of between £3.6m and £5.4m."[34]

There is a range of objections to this policy. In the first place, it is not obvious that "hybridization" (inter-species mating) is undesirable in itself. The statement that "hybridisation is recognised as the most significant threat to the species' [white-headed duck's] long-term survival"[35] is an odd kind of claim since in human terms we would hardly regard inter-racial marriage as a "threat" to the "survival" of one or both races. But, accepting for the sake of argument that hybridiza-tion is undesirable, and that "control" is therefore necessary, it still does not follow that *lethal* control is justifiable. Moreover, while the CBD may require the British Government to act, it is by no means clear that a variety of non-lethal controls could not be utilized.[36]

Consider: through no fault of its own (since it was intro-duced by human agencies) the ruddy duck, having adapted successfully to its new environment, is now going to be ruth-lessly exterminated over a period of six years, involving the infliction of incalculable suffering, at the expense of millions of pounds to the British taxpayer. And all this to preserve what is little more than a kind of species purity. But the most alarming fact of all is this: while we often expect govern-ments to be morally regressive when it comes to environmen-tal issues, in this case it was conservationists and ecologists, including the RSPB, who were unanimously in support of the killing, while opposition came principally from animal protection organizations.[37]

The second example is similar, and concerns the attempt to "control" the numbers of grey squirrels. This is proposed, among other things, in order to protect the red squirrel. DEFRA says that "it is widely (though not universally) accepted by the scientific and ecological communities that the presence of grey squirrels is inimical to reds and that if numbers of greys go unchecked reds will die out."[38] When asked what evidence there is that control by killing is effective, DEFRA responds by stating that "removal by killing is bound to be effective, if it is successful."[39] Of course, "removal by killing" is bound to be effective, but the fact is that killing does not always, if ever, totally remove a species unless the species is entirely elimi-nated by killing. We know that all animals breed in relation to the food and environment available. Killing may dent a popu-lation, but unless the entire population (in a definable area) is disposed of, the animals breed more frequently to compen-sate for their loss. Hence, killing is not always effective, and can even result over time in an *increased* population. What is true for squirrels is equally true for ruddy ducks. It is by no means clear that killing—even regular kills over a prolonged period of time—will always result in a substantial reduction, let alone elimination.

Consider: the British Government through public funds continues to deploy a policy of killing grey squirrels, supposedly (in part) to "protect" red squirrels through programs of "targeted control" leading to "local eradication." But when asked how many need to be killed, by whom, and over what timescale, DEFRA informs us that the "Forestry Commission [a government department responsible for the administration of forests and woodlands] ceased collation of data on the number of squirrels killed in woodland about ten years ago so we have no current data on numbers actually killed."[40] This admission is remarkable, and undermines all claims to control squirrels by killing. Calculating squirrel populations is itself problematic, but not even counting the numbers killed means that all justifications for control are devoid of a scientific basis.

No wonder that DEFRA says that "unless grey squirrel populations are permanently and naturally reduced by some other factor (such as disease) or our research uncovers another method of reducing populations, we believe that control by killing is an *indefinite* commitment where a landowner or manager decides it is merited."[41] Note the word "indefinite" here. Killing without end and, it seems, without evidence as to its effectiveness. Again, the most alarming fact of all is that conservationists and ecologists are among the first to defend such killing, even, as in this case, when there is insufficient empirical evidence to make a reasoned judgment.

These two cases alone expose how ready ecologists are to countenance the killing of wild animals and the insubstantial nature of their putative justifications. But counter questions may be asked: Do animal people not neglect or overlook the whole? Are they so concerned with the welfare of individuals that they fail to see the common (ecological) good? Does not an obsessive concern for individuals undercut the working out of ecological responsibility? Well, in the two cases I've cited (and many others I could mention), the undercutting is all one way. I know of no animal advocate who opposes ecological schemes save those that harm animals—and that is the rub. Injury to individual sentients should, and could in most cases, be avoided. Even in utilitarian terms, it is doubtful whether the "purity" of one species of duck could justify the destruction of five thousand other ducks, or whether the "protection" of the red squirrel could merit the "indefinite" killing of thousands of grey ones. It is not self-evident that we maintain the good of the whole by the destruction of individual parts.

It is important to see, however, that the apparent disagreements over killing and "management" are not just about the value of individual sentients, significant though that is. They concern much deeper issues about how humans should understand themselves in the world of creation. Whilst animal theologians are keen for humans to be pro-active in defense of threatened individual sentients, their overwhelming concern is to let creation be. They look askance at human attempts to control, manipulate and dominate more and more of the natural world, as if salvation consisted in human management of creation. Rather the hubris involved in such management is itself in need of salvation. Animal theologians do not deny that "made in the image of God" means that sometimes humans have to intervene (normally to rectify—as in the case of ruddy ducks—previous human mismanagement), or that sometimes difficult choices have to be made about the killing of individual sentients (despite what is said in the media, very few animal advocates believe that either human or animal rights are absolute), but such intervention requires explicit justification and a much greater sense of humility. The *imago dei* does not confer infallibility.

In the cases cited, what characterizes human involvement is the unquestioned assumption that humans always know better and that we alone can properly judge what is in the interest of creation or know how nature "really" ought to work. Despite years of disastrous mismanagement, humans still go on—now increasingly under the guise of ecological responsibility—wanting to subject more and more of the natural world to our designs of how it should be. Acknowledging past mistakes only serves the impetus to manage more, instead of acting as a warning against all meddling. It is paradoxical, to say the least, that a philosophy that emerged in a newly found sensibility to nature should issue in a more and more tyrannous attempt to control it. In conclusion, I have tried—from my admittedly partial perspective—to provide an account of the divergence of perception that underlies the current tension between animal and ecological theologians, and to show how this tension results in sharp divergences over practical issues. There is, I believe, no easy way to harmonize these perspectives. No, it is not essential that they should be in conflict. Theoretically it could, surely *must*, be possible to care for "the whole," as well as (or at least not to the detriment of) its "individual parts." But any attempt at harmonization really must begin by recognizing the deep theological cleavage that separates these two perceptions. Some really do look at Nature, perhaps sigh a little, but then offer thanksgiving, whilst others see only suffering that any decent Creator God must long to redeem.

I have one emollient thought to offer. The enduring value of theology to thinking about animals and ecology consists in a recognition that God relativizes all our human perceptions. If we have not "seen" this then all our visions will be hopelessly partial. Theology promises a God-centered rather than a human-centered view of the world. We cannot simply assume that our perspective is God's perspective. That recognition alone should give us all pause, even hope, that there is yet more to "see."

5

Responding to the Debate about Animal Theology

The National Association of Baptist Professors of Religion in the USA selected my book Animal Theology *for special study at their meeting at the Annual Assembly of the American Academy of Religion in Atlanta, Georgia in November 2003. Three scholars, Dr. David M. May, Professor of New Testament at the Central Baptist Theological Seminary in Kansas City, Missouri, Dr. Mark McEntire, Associate Professor of Religion at Belmont University in Nashville, Tennessee, and Dr. Sally Smith Holt, Assistant Professor of Religion at William Jewell College in Liberty, Missouri, provided detailed critiques from New Testament, Old Testament, and systematic theological perspectives. These were subsequently published, together with a lengthy response from myself, which is reproduced below, in the Baptist theological journal* Review & Expositor, 102/1 (Winter 2005), *in a special edition on animals and creation, titled "The Peaceable Kingdom." I am immensely grateful to my interlocutors for the honor they bestowed in giving my work their serious attention.*

Academics are a peculiar lot. Most of us are insecure, querulous, and difficult (some more than others), and we love recognition, scholarly prizes, and the approbation of the world. But the one thing we most crave (yet seldom receive) is the critical attention of our peers. I am, therefore, more than grateful to Professors May, McEntire, and Smith Holt for providing this particular blessing, and especially to Professor Nancy deClaissé-Walford, Vice-President of the National Association of Baptist Professors and Managing Editor of *Review*

& *Expositor*, for her daring (and uncommon perspicacity) in bringing this subject to light in the first place.

Like all true blessings, however, it is not entirely un-mixed. For while there is penetration and insight, some comments indicate how badly I have expressed myself, or made my *modus operandi* unclear. "You haven't understood me" is of course the claim of all rogues (and not a few academics), but in some instances it has plausibility, as I want to show.

I

Let me begin with David May's review. He discerns that for the subject to be "recognized by biblical scholars, and to impact Sunday-afternoon-fried-chicken Christians, it will need to find a voice that is more thorough in biblical exegesis and more openly biblically integrated." He may be right about some biblical scholars, though it is discomforting how little excellent biblical scholarship seems to impact upon the perspectives, let alone the moral actions, of biblical scholars, to say nothing of fried-chicken-eating Christians. Robert Murray's *The Cosmic Covenant*,[1] the most detailed biblical work to date—which uncovers strong animal-friendly voices in scripture—seems to have been passed over with hardly a whisper. And neither is that an isolated example. May obviously fancies that "thorough" and "integrated" scholarship most influences biblical scholars, among others. Oh that the world of academe was that straightforward—or just! May writes that "A thorough exegetical analysis of animal narratives in the New Testament would supply the foundation for a "faithful reading of the biblical text," which hopefully would cause *metanoia* in our thoughts and for our actions." The word "hopefully" is doing a lot of work in that sentence.

The assumption seems to be that if we get a "faithful reading" that is "thorough in biblical analysis and more biblically integrated," liberation (for animals) will be close at hand, or, at least, thoughtful engagement. It may be that such a book can be written, and that May has just the necessary scholarship and expertise (which sadly I lack) to do it. I wholeheartedly wish him well and offer every encouragement.

But, unlike him (and here I indicate my own confessional standpoint), I do not think that there is a "thorough" and "integrated" biblical analysis that will unambiguously provide an animal rights Bible. Nor a human rights Bible either, for that matter. On both issues there are positive and negative biblical insights, and, when it comes to animals, it is counter-intuitive to think that such culturally influenced documents (as I take all the biblical material to be) could possibly *unambiguously* support one line or another. And for obvious reasons: however inspired, the Bible is written by human beings for human beings, and it reflects, among other things, humanocentric views on animals. And, whilst it is capable of offering more than human insights, it originated in societies that held overwhelmingly instrumentalist views of animals. It is ungenerous to biblical revelation to suppose that it can entirely jump out of its cultural inheritance.

What is astonishing, however, is that given these obvious constraints, the biblical writers do sometimes articulate other than instrumentalist insights about animals. And I try to do justice to some of these in *Animal Theology*. But I do not claim to exhaust them, and I do not pretend that they represent, unequivocally or unambiguously, "*the* biblical view." Perhaps May thinks there is such a thing.

But it is unfair to characterize my exegesis as a "proof-text method" or even "favorite text-segments" analysis. My work has been well trodden and acquitted of that charge.[2] Neither do I accept Malina's distinction between using scripture as a "warrant for agendas instead of a witness." A witness, properly heard, *constitutes* an agenda. Under the tutelage and inspiration of Karl Barth, I have been profoundly influenced by the biblical "witness,"[3] which, in reality, is many, even contradictory, witnesses. Nowhere is this clearer than in the practice of eating meat. While I tentatively attempt a harmonization of Genesis 1 and 9 (the only place I do so in the book), I desist elsewhere. Unlike May, I am generally untrusting of "integration"—by which I fear (perhaps unfairly) he means harmonization. It may be that diversity, even and especially in scripture, is more reflective of triune diversity than we admit.

We cannot get away from the problem of finding a vantage point from which we are to see—and interpret. Not all biblical texts unambiguously serve moral causes, even and especially our favorite ones; some insights have to be primary. *Animal Theology* stands or falls by whether I have grasped some of the important biblical insights that should be at the heart of this debate. The most significant of these is the generosity of God disclosed in the life of Jesus Christ. I may not have selected the most pertinent texts, or given them the most thoughtful exposition; but that Jesus offers us a model of lordship manifest in service—a paradigm of inclusive moral generosity to those normally beyond the boundaries of moral concern—is, I contend, pure Gospel, and its implications are vast for re-envisaging Christian theology in relation to our "dominion" over animals.

II

Mark McEntire also appears to accept the moral ambiguity of scripture:

> Unfortunately, the major ideas of *Animal Theology* seem utterly foreign to the Old Testament. This is in no way a rejection of Linzey's program. We should recognize that an idea like the abolition of slavery also seems foreign to the Old Testament. The best we might say is that the command to love neighbor as self in Leviticus 19:18 created a momentum that cannot be ultimately resisted, even if it takes thousands of years to overcome an entrenched institution like slavery.

We now take as a given that slavery is incompatible with the Christian Gospel. But the reason for this presumed incompatibility has much less to do with Leviticus than it has with an implicit acceptance of the model of inclusive moral generosity glimpsed in Jesus. Some abolitionist campaigners said so explicitly.[4] But, if this is to be the revisionist, hermeneutical principle, it has implications beyond slavery, or indeed women.

Yet it is astonishing that the major ideas of *Animal Theology* are deemed "utterly foreign to the Old Testament."

Consider: animals are God's creatures, that is, they have a worth independent of human wants and needs. How different is this from the modern philosophy of animal rights, which speaks of animals having "intrinsic value"? Consider further: animals are expressly included in the Noahic covenant. At the very least, this implies a common bond between humans, animals, and their Creator. How different is this from the idea found in modern literature on animal ethics that there is a "kinship" between sentient creatures, and that the lives of other sentient species should be respected? Again: humans are made in God's image and given power to look after animals as God's deputies, which implies, at the very least, a profound responsibility to other species. How different is this from contemporary animal philosophy, which holds that humans alone are moral agents who should acknowledge duties to animals, which they cannot acknowledge towards us?

McEntire says "our use of animals is deeply entrenched in human culture," and was so in biblical times. Quite so. That is why it is remarkable that people who were not pacifists, vegetarians, or opponents of capital punishment felt so keenly the incongruity between violence and their belief in a holy, loving Creator—so much so that they conceived that God must have created a world free of it. That is the insight which lies behind Genesis 1:29–30: "I give you all plants that bear the seed everywhere on earth, and every tree bearing fruit which yields seed: they shall be yours for food." It is *that* creation—a wholly vegetarian, nonviolent creation—that God describes as "very good."

As I have written elsewhere:

> The notion, then, that violence between creatures is not what God originally intended is not some latest form of animal-rights propaganda. On the contrary, it can lay claim to form part of one of the earliest strands of biblical reflection. Animal advocates have not invented a world in which God makes us and all creation vegetarian; neither have they invented a world in which the lion lays down with the lamb. Both insights are given in the Judaeo-Christian tradition and rekindled afresh

in a new generation. Far from modern advocacy diminishing biblical insights, in crucial respects it depends upon them.[5]

McEntire says that I use the Genesis 1 text, and also Isaiah 11, to argue that "the biblical writers looked forward to a time in the future when killing would no longer be necessary," when "God's original will for all creation" would be restored. He asks: "Who among us does not hope that he is right about this, of course?" But this is not a question of whether Linzey is "right," but rather of attending to the eschatological hope of both the Old and New Testaments. This is not a question of "favorite text-segments" as May claims, but rather of encountering in scripture the living God who is both Creator and Redeemer. The characteristic thrust of the biblical writers is eschatological—to look forward to what God will do in the future, to complete the work of creation by grace.

No, human beings cannot achieve the Kingdom by meritorious works alone, but we can be sure that God's will is for a transformed creation. At the very least, an ethical vegetarianism (desisting from killing when we have no need to do so) is an act of anticipation of the peaceable Kingdom that we seek, and this may be the most we can claim of any ethical endeavor. Yes, we can argue about the details of who or what will be included, and in precisely what way, but that the God disclosed in Jesus Christ seeks the transformation of the entire creation is so central to biblically oriented thinking that it engenders despair that biblical scholars do not immediately grasp it.

McEntire argues that "Linzey's ethic of generosity may help to sustain the momentum to overcome it [our entrenched use of animals], but *one searches in vain for the Old Testament text to provide the necessary power to start the process*" (my emphasis). Really? To take just one example, the Hebrew Bible does not envisage that we have an unlimited dominion over animals. The various humane provisions in Hebrew law (see, for example, Leviticus 22:28, Deuteronomy 41:21, Deuteronomy 22:10, Exodus 23:5, Deuteronomy 22:1),[6] whilst not a charter for positive animal rights, at least suppose, negatively, that we do not have absolute rights. Even within a culture deeply indebted to animal use, there is an emerging sense of moral limits. From these various injunctions, Judaism developed its own biblically based principle of not unnecessarily causing suffering to animals—a principle that, while neglected and often stated in a weaker rather than a stronger form, informed anti-cruelty movements up until the last century.[7]

McEntire claims that I separate Isaiah 11:6–9 from 1–5, "a mistake made by many who use this text." It is true I do not refer to it but, in context, it entirely reinforces my thesis. He says that the picture of the "ideal king" in verse 4b ("he [God] shall strike the earth with the rod of his mouth, and with the breath of his lips he shall kill the wicked") is "devastating." Well, it is not "devastating" to my thesis. The divine rod of righteousness (not gratuitous punishment) exercised upon the wicked is essential to those who believe in ultimate judgment for human beings because of their violent and wicked ways. Humans constitute the moral rot of the universe, so that only divine intervention, mediated or not, can bring it to an end. Only then, finally, will the lamb lie down with the wolf.

McEntire comments on 11:1–5 that "humanity has laboured fruitlessly for millennia to achieve peace through violence, not realizing that any such project is doomed from the beginning," but he fails to see that Isaiah is referring here not to human agency per se but to divine agency. *God's* justice—to which Isaiah's words poetically and metaphorically point—is utterly different from the sinful human desire for revenge or conquest.

III

Sally Smith Holt seems less than persuaded that incarnation is "for" all creation (as I put it, following Barth, God's "yes" to all creation), but *Animal Theology* little more than attenuates the thrust of patristic doctrine. Unless we are to be absurdly literal and say that the incarnation is only God's "yes" to one particular man in history (and not women or other creatures), it must follow that the incarnation is God's love affair with all flesh. This is not some radical Linzeyist interpretation, but follows from appreciating that all creation is interrelated, as Pope John Paul II makes clear:

> [The incarnation] signifies the taking up into unity with God not only human nature but in this human nature, in a sense, everything that is flesh, the whole of humanity, the entire visible world. The incarnation . . . also has a cosmic dimension.[8]

Holt argues that this assumption "requires us to believe that animals are in *need* of redemption" (her emphasis), and she asks whether they are "in need of redemption *in the same way* that humans are in need of redemption" (my emphasis), claiming that "Linzey does not give a clear answer." But throughout the book, I repeat my view that animals are not moral agents with free will, and are not therefore capable of sin. Redemption for animals will therefore be different from human redemption. Indeed, from a theological perspective, human redemption is altogether more problematic since animals are not sinful, faithless, and wicked in the way in which humans are.

But the notion of redemption is still appropriate for animals because they need to be saved both from the effects of human cruelty and also from the natural "cruelty" exhibited in the parasitical nature of creation. The challenging biblical insight is that human and animal redemption are intimately related. Following St. Paul (Romans 8:18–24), while the Christian view has frequently been focused on the centrality of humanity in creation, "it may yet be possible, in ways we scarcely understand, for creation to free itself from bondage by humans releasing themselves from their own." No, humans cannot redeem animals (only God can do that), but they can at least become anticipatory signs of the Kingdom—even, perhaps, "co-participants and co-workers with God in the redemption of the world."[9]

Paul's conception of creation in bondage awaiting the "first [human] fruits" of redemption by God is a bold and demanding vision. But it is fed by the realization that parasitical nature is un-Christ-like. Some Christians have difficulties enough in trying to conceive of redeemed human beings, let alone a creation free of predation and parasitism, but it is precisely that vision—of a peaceful creation in which the big fish greets the little fish and does *not* eat it—that is required if we are to believe in a holy, loving God, Creator and Redeemer, who does, in the end, make all things new. There is a stark challenge here for modern theology, and one that has not been grasped by those who write in a wholly humanocentric way about the nature of evil. Either parasitical nature is or is not evil. Either God wills a self-murdering system of survival or God does not. There really is not a third way.

Holt should not be surprised that I do not go the way of process or ecotheologians, like Rosemary Radford Ruether, Jay B. McDaniel, and Sallie McFague, since all of them seem united in accepting predation as God's will. Smith says that "McFague maintains that God is incarnated in the world as she imagines the world as the body of God," and therefore "redemption for animals is unnecessary." Quite so, but *that* is the problem. God is so identified with the world, indeed coterminous with it, that it is difficult to see how God could be the Redeemer either for animals *or* humans.

Holt says that my thought detracts from McFague's "idea of the world as sacred." Quite so. Ecotheologians who think that they can re-value animals and creation by "sacralizing" them inhibit a proper conception of God as Creator and Redeemer, and so befuddle theology. Creation has intrinsic value to God, but it is not "sacred"—it is not divine. Smith thinks ecotheologians' and my "goals are similar." They are not. Only a fully Trinitarian God—Father, Son, and Holy Spirit; Creator, Redeemer, and Sanctifier—both immanent and transcendent, is capable of bringing about the world-transforming redemption which is the goal of Christian eschatology. The logic is inescapable: no real state of fallenness, no real redemption. A God who cannot be a Redeeming God in relation to animals turns out not to be God at all.[10]

How we explain the fact that animals, who have no free will, live in a state of fallenness subject to the evil of predation is no easy matter. Elsewhere I have given an account of the problem and, with the assistance of C. S. Lewis, explored some possible answers.[11] Some Christians have difficulty in believing in cosmic disorder, let alone a source of cosmic evil, present in the world before the arrival of dinosaurs and human beings. That view certainly has its problems, but it is theologically essential if we are to believe that predation is not willed by the Creator. The alternative is dire beyond words, for it involves accepting that the "natural world" is actually God's creation as first intended and, as a corollary, that death, disease, decay, and predation are actually God's will for all living beings. Is this compatible with the God revealed in Jesus Christ? I shall try, humorously (and therefore very seriously), to indicate what the "anti-Gospel of Jesus our predator" might actually look like:

> Jesus, according to the Predator Gospel, would be the butcher par excellence. He would be the one who, far from desisting from animal sacrifice, actually encouraged his disciples to excel in it. Instead of driving out the sacrificial animals from the Temple, the Jesus of the Predator Gospel would drive them in. The line that most characterises his ministry would not be "the good shepherd lays down his life for the sheep" but rather "the good shepherd slaughters—with gratitude—as many sheep as he can." Far from beginning his ministry, according to Mark (1:13), "with the wild beasts" and thereby symbolising reconciliation with nature, the Predator Jesus would be "with the wild beasts" with bow and arrow. Instead of commending the rescuing of a fallen animal from the pit, Predator Jesus would point to the inevitability of God's far-reaching plan of death, disease, and decay. . . .
>
> Since predation is [according to ecotheologians] God's blessing, the predator Jesus would offer a singular example in the human realm too. Far from consorting with sinners or excusing prostitutes, the Predator Jesus would be the first to cast the stone. Instead of healing the sick, the Predator Jesus could only approve of the efficacy of God-given ecological systems. Instead of raising Lazarus from the dead, the Predator Jesus could only comment that death is God's blessing. Instead of preaching the good news of the coming kingdom of God, the proclamation would run [in the words of Matthew Fox]: "Eat and be eaten."[12]

As a sideline, Bishop John A. T. Robinson, on learning that he had cancer, told newspaper reporters that "God is in the cancer as he is in everything else." A thousand times "no," I say. How could a New Testament scholar have lived so long with the Gospel stories of Jesus and simply failed to grasp the existential reality of the demonic? If biblical scholars cannot see the evil of cancer (an organism that lives only by causing its own death, and that of its host), then we should not be surprised if they do not also respond to the innocent, even Christ-like, suffering of animals.

Holt, predictably, questions my view that animals have rights. Predictably, because here, more than anywhere else, my thought has been misrepresented by commentators.[13] Holt views my work (as most commentators do) through the work of secular theorists, such as Peter Singer and Tom Regan, and then assumes that I have simply taken over their ideas or reflect their thought. But I have to point out (however immodest it may appear) that my first work, *Animal Rights: A Christian Perspective* (1976) was published in the United Kingdom before Peter Singer's *Animal Liberation* (1977), and eight years before Tom Regan's *The Case for Animal Rights* (1984). Unaware of the extent of the Linzey corpus, commentators simply assume that I am serving up secular thought in some Christian guise. I am happy to acknowledge my debt (in some respects) to these thinkers (as I do in print), but actually I am on a very different track and do not come with (or agree with) much of the philosophical baggage that accompanies them.

Therefore, when Holt says "this is the foundation [secular rights theory] from which he [Linzey] moves to consideration of *theos*-rights," that is true but only in one sense. My *Animal Rights* contains a critique of the traditional criteria for awarding rights (personhood, rationality, soul possession) and proposes sentiency as an alternative criterion, and is, therefore, heavily philosophical. But subsequently in *Christianity and the Rights of Animals* (1987), I develop at length what was implicit in my earlier work, namely that the rights of the creature must be based on the rights of the Creator to have what is created treated with respect (what I term "*theos*-rights"). For the record, then, I would be obliged if I was not just lumped together with other secular "rights theorists," because even if the positions which some of them now advocate were those I myself anticipated (or advocated) way back in 1976, since then I have increasingly developed a specifically theological perspective on animals, rights, and creation.[14]

Not infrequently, commentators reading me assume that they have found some deficiency in my thought because I have failed to touch upon such and such a problem or respond to this or that particular issue. But the truth is that I have written so much (twenty books and 180 articles) that someone entering the corpus from the perspective of one, or even two books fails to appreciate (despite notes) the range of previous work. Thus, for example, complaints that "Linzey's sentiency criterion is rather ambiguous because he does not determine its boundaries in relation to animals," and that "Linzey fails . . . to clearly identify what life forms have this capability" overlook previous discussion of these issues.[15]

My view, then, is that animals have God-given rights. But it is vital to grasp the theological logic underpinning this position: Animals are God's creatures, they have intrinsic value not just as collectivities but as individuals. The Spirit is the source of their life and some creatures are endowed with God-given capacities for intelligence and sentiency. Humans are made in God's image and we are given power over animals, which, Christologically interpreted, is the power of God to care for them as God himself cares. As I have already said, in speaking of their "rights" we conceptualize what we owe to them objectively as a matter of justice because they are God's creatures.

Rights language, as I explain in *Animal Theology*, needs to be theologically qualified. In an absolute sense, there can be no rights of the creature against the Creator, but as sovereign Creator, God has the fundamental right to see that what is created is treated with respect. There is a downside to the use of rights language, especially in a secular context where it can be viewed as little more than an extension of negotiating moral goods. It is also vital to understand that, from a theological perspective, rights language is never enough—rights only delineate moral limits, which we should not (normally) pass in our treatment of the non-human. But, in addition to rights, we should also utilize other vocabulary, such as generosity, care, gentleness, love, welfare, and protection, since no one concept says everything that could, or should, be said about our moral obligations to animals.

Nevertheless, rights language does have some advantages, and one especially from a theological perspective. It helps us to articulate more adequately *God's own interest* in the lives of other sentient creatures. Animal rights, properly understood, are *"theos*-rights"—God's own rights, not something owned, won, or granted by one creature to another. That is why Holt's strictures about rights are so off-beam, and why, specifically, the language of duties which she (like many others) seems to prefer is so often inadequate. For the danger of duties (even the language of generosity, which I also espouse) is that it locates the source of obligation within ourselves, and thereby fails to see that *God's own right* is objectively involved in the way we treat animals.

In conclusion: of the making of many arguments there is no end, and lest anyone should be unmoved by our academic wrangling, let me reiterate that there are serious theological issues at stake. Over the years, I have moved from thinking that animals are a serious, if rather secondary, issue in theology to seeing that they constitute a test of the adequacy of theology itself. As I have written elsewhere:

> . . . the promise of real theology has always been that it will liberate us from humanocentrism, that is from a purely human view of the world to a truly God-centred one. Theology at its best has always claimed to be more than a purely human view of the world. Once grasped, the issue of animals is seen for what it is: a central test of the adequacy of Christian theology and its claim to offer an objective God-centred account of the world including some account of the purpose, meaning and value of the other non-human creatures. To go on supposing that the meaning and value of other creatures can be determined solely by their relationship with human beings is

untheological. Confronting [our prejudices about animals], then, is not about Christian theology's latest concession to secular fashion, it is an imperative derived from the heart of theology's mission: to render a truthful, non-partial account of the creation God has made.[16]

Jesus and Animals

A Different Perspective

As we have seen, it is not long before discussions of animal theology center on the issue of Jesus and his attitude toward animals. In addition to the canonical Gospels, there are also many "apocryphal" accounts, which provide a rather different perspective. Five segments of texts are analyzed here that reveal a remarkable interest in motifs that relate to our kinship with animals, living peaceably with them, and their compassionate treatment. It is significant that there were early portrayals of the life of Jesus that understood his ministry to be inclusive of the animal world. I would not have researched this area without the encouragement of Laura Moretti who commissioned me to write for the Christianity section of her Animal Voice *website at <www.godandanimals.com/PAGES/edits/linsey.html>. A revised version titled: "Jesus and Animals in Early Apocryphal Literature" was also published in* Modern Believing *(January 2007).*

It is often claimed that Jesus said virtually nothing about animals, and that Christian thought has been indifferent or hostile to animal welfare. In fact, there is a long tradition of Christian thought about animals. Early "apocryphal" Christian literature, from the first to the eighth centuries, often developed and embellished canonical Gospel accounts of Jesus' relations with animals. The term "apocryphal" requires some explanation. As is well known, the early Church selected the documents (Gospels and letters) that it regarded as authoritative for the Christian community. These documents are now known as the New Testament that, together with the Old Testament, constitutes the "canon" of Christian scripture. In this process, some books were left out or disregarded because they were thought to be inadequate doctrinally, or plainly heretical. But a considerable quantity of material was regarded as more or less orthodox but less authoritative than others. "Apocryphal," therefore, does not necessarily mean unorthodox or unreliable; it simply means that, given the understanding of the time, they were thought to be less acceptable than others.

There is a voluminous amount of Christian literature that was not selected by the early Church but that is nonetheless interesting in providing insights into how Christians once thought and felt. A sizeable proportion of this material relates directly or indirectly to animals. In what follows, I select five segments of texts that focus on Jesus' own relations with animals, and offer a theological commentary on them:

1. Jesus' healing of a mule (Coptic fragment);
2. The catalepsy of all creation at Jesus' birth (The Proto-evangelium of James);
3. Jesus creates the sparrows (The Infancy Gospel of Thomas);
4. The birth of Jesus with animals (The Gospel of Pseudo-Matthew);
5. Jesus—the harbinger of peace to the animal world (The Gospel of Pseudo-Matthew).

1. Jesus' healing of a mule (Coptic fragment)

It happened that the Lord left the city and walked with his disciples over the mountains. And they came to a mountain, and the road which led up it was steep. There they found a man with a pack-mule. But the animal had fallen, because the man had loaded it too heavily, and now he beat it, so that it was bleeding. And Jesus came to him and said, "Man, why do you beat your animal? Do you not see that it is too weak for its burden, and do you not know that it suffers pains?" But the man answered and said, "What is that to you? I may beat it as much as I please, since it is my property, and I bought it for a good sum of money. Ask those who are with you, for they know me and they know about this." And some of the disciples said, "Yes, Lord, it is as he says. We have seen how he bought it." But the Lord said, "Do you then not see how it bleeds, and do you not hear how it groans and cries out?" But they answered and said, "No, Lord, that it groans and cries out, we do not hear." But Jesus was sad and exclaimed, "Woe to you, that you do not hear how it complains to the Creator in heaven and cries out for mercy. But threefold woes to him about whom it cries out and complains in its pain." And he came up and touched the animal. And it stood up and its wounds were healed. But Jesus said to the man, "Now carry on and from now on do not beat it any more, so that you too may find mercy."

Precisely how old is the story of Jesus' healing of a mule, or its exact source, is difficult to determine. The above translation is by Richard Bauckham of a version in an earlier collection of Coptic texts first translated into German by J. Boehmer in 1903, who simply lists it under the heading "Coptic Bible."[1] According to Roderick Dunkerley, who translated the text in 1957, it is entirely in keeping "with the Spirit of the Gospels" and "since kindness to animals was an aspect of Christian charity which the Early Church largely ignored" this may account for "such an incident falling out of notice."[2]

Bauckham maintains that the story presupposes the Jewish legal tradition concerning the injunction to relieve an animal fallen under its burden (Exodus 23:4; Deuteronomy 22:4), "so the story may go back to a Jewish-Christian source in which Jesus' teaching that love is the overriding principle in interpreting the law was extended, as it is not explicitly in the canonical Gospels, to concern for animals as well as people."[3] We cannot disregard the possibility that the text itself contains genuine historical reminiscence and therefore relates to an actual event in the life of Jesus. It needs to be remembered that even later texts may contain elements of much earlier material, so that even texts dating from the fourth or fifth centuries may be more trustworthy than might be supposed.

What is significant is that this fragment, preserved in Coptic, illustrates that some early Christians saw Jesus' ethic as extending to the care of suffering animals. The animal concerned cries out to its Creator for mercy, suggesting that the animal also has its own relationship with God who hears its cries. But it is the failure of human beings to respond compassionately to the cries of the creature that most invites Jesus' consternation and rebuke. Indeed, there is something contemporary, even prophetic, in Jesus' rebuke to those around him who apparently fail to hear the cries of the suffering animal. The uncomprehending response, "No, Lord, that it [the mule] groans and cries out, we do not hear," earns a "threefold woe" that those who should hear apparently do not. As Bauckham points out, Jesus' attitude exemplifies the general principle that "the measure you give will be the measure you get" (Matthew 7:2; Luke 6:38), as well as the thought of the beatitude: "Blessed are the merciful, for they will receive mercy" (Matthew 5:7)."[4]

The text, therefore, unambiguously invites us to picture Jesus as compassionate to animals, even as a healer of their suffering. Perhaps Dunkerley is right; *that* thought was deemed so radical that it helps explain why the text was jettisoned at an early stage. Nevertheless, the message so coheres with other aspects of the teaching and ministry of Jesus that it is difficult to deny its prima facie authenticity. One cannot help wondering whether there are other, yet to be translated, texts (Coptic and others) similarly buried away in libraries that support this more inclusive view of Jesus' ministry.

2. The catalepsy of all creation at Jesus' birth (The Proto-evangelium of James)

According to the Proto-evangelium account of the catalepsy of all creation, Joseph finds a cave (not a stable) for Mary to rest and goes in search of a midwife for his heavily pregnant wife. He recounts that as he was walking a strange event took place:

Now I, Joseph, was walking, and yet I did not walk. And I looked up into the air and saw the air in amazement. And I looked up at the vault of heaven, and saw it standing still and the birds of heaven motionless. And I looked down at the earth, and saw a dish placed there and workmen reclining, and their hands were in the dish. But those who chewed did not chew, and those who lifted up

*did not lift, and those who put something to their mouth put noth-
ing to their mouth, but everyone looked upwards. And behold,
sheep were being driven and they did not come forward but stood
still; and the shepherd raised his hands to strike them with his staff
but his hand remained upright. And I looked at the flow of the
river, and saw the mouths of kids over it and they did not drink.
And then suddenly everything went on its course.*[5]

At first sight the meaning of this strange experience might
appear rather opaque; that is, until one appreciates that the
author is seeking to describe how the birth of Jesus affects the
entire created order. The truth revealed in this poetic way is
that the event of this one birth has cosmic significance—for
everything that lives. The earth stands still, as it were, to greet
its redeemer in human form. Of course, nature miracles are
not unknown in the New Testament and this event has obvious parallels with the reported earthquake and eclipse at the
time of Jesus' crucifixion, for example in Matthew where Jesus'
death is attended by strange events including the shaking of
the earth and the opening of tombs (Matthew 27:51–3).

According to J. K. Elliott, the Proto-evangelium is one of
the most influential of the apocryphal Gospels and dates from
about the second half of the second century, though, here
again, it is possible that it is considerably earlier, or at least
contains an earlier stratum of material.[6] The interest in creation is typical of much apocryphal material and is lyrically
expressed in the Song of Anna (Mary's mother), who compares her barrenness to the created fruitfulness of the earth,
and especially the other creatures:

> Woe is me, to what am I likened?
> I am not likened to the birds of heaven,
> For even the birds of heaven are fruitful before you, O
>   Lord.

> Woe is me, to what am I likened?
> I am not likened to the beasts of the earth,
> For even the beasts of the earth are fruitful before you,
>   O Lord.

I am not likened to this earth,
For even this earth brings forth its fruit in its season and
   praises you, O Lord.[7]

The song celebrates fecundity as God's gift to all living
creatures, and contrasts her own position with the perfect
fulfillment of God's purpose in non-human creatures. Since
fertility and fruitfulness were associated with righteousness
(see Psalm 1:1–6), the implication is that non-human creatures reflect God's will and receive God's blessing in a way in
which she cannot. The song itself is prefaced by Anna's obser-
vation of "a nest of sparrows"[8] and concludes by emphasizing
the praise of the creatures for their Creator. It is a beautifully
"earthy" song, entirely appropriate for a Gospel whose infancy
narratives speak of the mystery of God made flesh.

3. Jesus creates the sparrows
(The Infancy Gospel of Thomas)

*When this boy Jesus was five years old he was playing at the cross-
ing of a stream, and he gathered together into pools the running
water, and instantly made it clean, and gave his command with
a single word. Having made soft clay he moulded from it twelve
sparrows. And it was the Sabbath when he did these things. And
there were also many other children playing with him. When
a certain Jew saw what Jesus was doing while playing on the
Sabbath, he at once went and told his father Joseph, "See, your
child is at the stream, and he took clay and moulded twelve
birds and has profaned the Sabbath." And when Joseph came
to the place and looked, he cried out to him, saying, "Why do
you do on the Sabbath things which it is not lawful to do?" But
Jesus clapped his hands and cried out to the sparrows and said
to them, "Be gone!" And the sparrows took flight and went away
chirping. The Jews were amazed when they saw this, and went
away and told their leaders what they had seen Jesus do.[9]*

It is possible that the Infancy Gospel of Thomas fills some gaps
in the childhood of Jesus up to twelve years old. Again, dating
is imprecise but sometime around the fifth century appears

likely. Elliott argues that the "theological teaching of these stories is minimal" and that the "main thrust of the episodes is to stress in a crudely sensational way the miraculous powers of Jesus."[10] But these incidents do convey a closeness with, even fellow feeling for animals that is only obliquely found in the canonical Gospels.

For example, in the passage above, Jesus is depicted as the miraculous creator of sparrows, which he makes out of clay in apparent contravention of Jewish law that forbade work on the Sabbath. Here the story resonates with two other incidents found in the canonical Gospels. The first concerns the saying of Jesus that even sparrows (*strouthia* in Greek: "little birds') are not forgotten by God (Luke 12:6–7), and the second concerns the principle enumerated by Jesus that it is "lawful to do good on the Sabbath," which by implication includes extending compassion to an animal fallen into a pit (see Matthew 12:10–12).

When linked with the story in the Infancy Gospel of Thomas, a line of interpretation emerges: God is the Creator of all life and Jesus is God's agent in creation, "begotten even before the creation of the world" as the Gospel of Thomas subsequently makes clear (para 7:1). Since the Creator delights in the creation of other beings, so Jesus' youthful activity imitates his Father's own creative work. This divine work of creation continues every day (even on the Sabbath) and takes precedence over any interpretation of religious laws of the time. Jesus' creation of sparrows not only reinforces his special relationship with the Creator and Father of all, but also demonstrates his closeness (as specific Creator) with the "little birds," which, like all beings, are created from the dust (or clay) of the earth. Indeed, the parallel with Genesis 2:7 is unmistakable: as God the Father creates man from the dust of the earth and breathes life into him, so Jesus (in this story) creates the sparrows from the dust and breathes on them likewise.

Elliott says that "the infancy stories represent the encapsulating in writing at various points in history of a developing cycle of oral tradition."[11] Whether this story stretches back in time to the actual life of Jesus is debatable and probably unprovable, but what is significant is that Jesus' interest in the life of other creatures is a consistent motif in the childhood

stories about him. In the same Gospel, other incidents reinforce this view. Jesus is reported to have healed his brother
James of a viper's bite, to have breathed on a dead fish to bring
it back to life, and, in a playful mood, causes twelve sparrows
to interfere with the instruction of his teacher.[12]

4. The birth of Jesus with animals
(The Gospel of Pseudo-Matthew)

*And on the third day after the birth of our Lord Jesus Christ,
Mary went out of the cave and, entering a stable, placed the child
in the manger, and an ox and an ass adored him. Then was fulfilled that which was said by Isaiah the prophet. "The ox knows
his owner, and the ass his master's crib." Therefore, the animals,
the ox and the ass, with him in their midst, incessantly adored
him. Then was fulfilled that which was said by Habakkuk the
prophet, saying "Between two animals you are made manifest."
Joseph remained in the same place with Mary for three days.*[13]

The tradition of Jesus being born in (or, in Pseudo-Matthew,
later transferred to) a stable accompanied by the animals is so
well known that most people assume that it is present in the
canonical Gospels. In fact, it is only in the Gospel of Pseudo-
Matthew that the animals are specifically mentioned. Their
existence may have been simply assumed in the canonical
accounts (the stable is specifically mentioned in Luke 2:7f.),
but in Pseudo-Matthew a theological rationale for their existence emerges: they are to greet the Christ-child and render
him adoration in conformity with Hebrew scriptures, specifically, Isaiah 1:3 and Habakkuk 3:2.

Although, according to Elliott, Pseudo-Matthew was popular during the Middle Ages, the tradition of animals at the birth
of Jesus may well have been older. Wilhelm Schneemelcher
reports that the ox and the ass appear on sarcophagi of the
fourth and fifth centuries and on ivory carvings of the fifth
and sixth centuries.[14] Pseudo-Matthew was apparently compiled in Latin in the eighth or ninth century, and may be an
embellishment of the tradition, or conceivably an earlier but
subsequently disregarded element of the original infancy nar-

ratives. Either way, it is impressive testimony to the idea that animals were there at the beginning, and to the insight (found elsewhere in apocryphal material) that animals participate in, if not herald, worship of the Christ-child.

Indeed, this theme is immediately continued in the text in a range of further dramatic stories. Approaching another cave, Mary and Joseph and their children encounter dragons who cause the children to flee, but Jesus, unafraid, meets the dragons who worship him. Jesus admonishes the dragons to hurt no one, and says to his fearful parents, "Do not be afraid; and do not consider me to be a child, for I am and always have been perfect; and all the beasts of the forest must needs be docile before me."[15] The incident apparently fulfills the prophecy in Psalm 148:7 that the Lord is praised "from the earth, dragons, and all you ocean depths."

5. Jesus—the harbinger of peace to the animal world (The Gospel of Pseudo-Matthew)

Other animals, lions and panthers, apparently accompany the Holy Family into the desert, "showing them the way and bowing their heads" and indicating "their submission by wagging their tails" and worshipping Jesus "with great reverence":

Now at first, when Mary saw the lions and the panthers and various kinds of wild beasts surrounding them, she was very much afraid. But the infant Jesus looked into her face with joyful countenance and said, "Be not afraid, mother, for they come not to do you harm, but they make haste to serve both you and me." With these words he drove all fear from her heart. And the lions kept walking with them, and with the oxen and the asses and the beasts of burden, which carried what they needed, and did not hurt a single one of them, though they remained with them; they were tame among the sheep and the rams which they had brought with them from Judea and which they had with them. They walked among wolves and feared nothing; and not one of them was hurt by another. Then was fulfilled that which was spoken by the prophet, "Wolves shall feed with lambs; lion and ox shall eat straw together."[16]

The last reference to Isaiah 65:25, when God shall renew the earth and establish peace between all creatures (as in Isaiah 11:1–9), makes explicit the messianic theme of peaceful co-existence in Jesus' period in the wilderness with the wild beasts in Mark 1:13. It is remarkable how the belief that the Messiah will bring peace to creation persisted and was perpetuated throughout years of Christian storytelling. Whether the events described in this story took place is rather beside the point; the point is that as Christians reflected upon the life and work of Jesus they became convinced that his work would issue in peace for all creation in fulfillment of the prophecies in Isaiah. Notice how both fear and violence are overcome in the story—all rather astonishing when it is appreciated that, in context, human beings lived with the real threat of being attacked by wild predators. Jesus' influence creates a life of harmonious, non-violent co-existence in which the wild animals—far from threatening or harming humans—are liberated into a new level of peaceableness both with their human neighbors and with fellow species.

Also worth attention is the apparent statement of Jesus in the previous passage that "I am and always have been perfect; and all the beasts of the forest must needs be docile before me." At first sight there appears to be no obvious connection between these ideas, namely of perfection and friendliness. It is only in the context of messianic prophecy that such a linkage makes sense. It is because Jesus is "perfect," that is, the Messiah sent by God to renew the earth, that he is recognized even, and especially, by the wild beasts. They recognize his authority as that of one who, unlike others, comes with genuine benevolence to heal the earth and usher in the peaceable kingdom. This idea is further exemplified in the subsequent story of Jesus, aged only eight years, and his encounter with the lions. It deserves to be read in full:

And there was beside the road, near the bank of Jordan, a cave where the lioness was nursing her whelps; and no one was safe to walk that way. Jesus, coming from Jericho, and knowing that in that cave the lioness had brought forth her young, went into it in the sight of all. And when the lions saw Jesus, they ran to meet

*him and worshipped him. And Jesus was sitting in the cavern
and the lion's whelps ran round his feet, fawning and playing
with him. And the older lions, with their heads bowed, stood at
a distance and worshipped him and fawned upon him with their
tails. Then the people who were standing afar off and who did not
see Jesus, said, "Unless he or his parents had committed grievous
sins, he would not of his own accord have exposed himself to the
lions." And when the people were reflecting within themselves
and were overcome with great sorrow, behold, suddenly in the
sight of the people Jesus came out of the cave and the lions went
before him, and the lion's whelps played with each other before
his feet. And the parents of Jesus stood afar off with their heads
bowed and watched; likewise also the people stood at a distance
on account of the lions, for they did not dare come close to them.
Then Jesus began to say to the people, "How much better are the
beasts than you, seeing that they recognise their Lord and glorify
him; while you men, who have been made in the image and likeness of God, do not know him! Beasts know me and are tame;
men see me and do not acknowledge me."*

After these things Jesus crossed the Jordan in the sight
of them all with the lions; and the water of the Jordan was
divided on the right hand and on the left. Then he said to the
lions so that all could hear, "Go in peace and hurt no one;
neither let man injure you, until you return to the place where
you have come from." And they, bidding him farewell, not only
with their voices but with their gestures, went to their own
place. But Jesus returned to his mother.[17]

The superiority of the animals (in recognizing Jesus and worshipping him) in contrast to humans is a exceptional idea given
the contexts in which these stories circulated; after all, it was
the common view throughout all centuries of Christian thought
that humans are superior to animals because they are made in
the image of God. Yet, here we have a story of Jesus, which circulated for decades, if not centuries, within the community of
Christian believers that expresses the idea that animals have a
spiritual capacity that supersedes humanity.

One possible source for this view may derive from the realization that while human beings are sinful, animals cannot

sin since they are not moral agents. According to Christian theology, humans alone are morally responsible because they have free will whereas animals have no such freedom. But the logical conclusion of this train of thought is that since animals cannot sin, they must be closer to the state of natural blessedness that God intended. Since their lives have not been disfigured by sin, they still possess an original innocence in a way that humans do not.

Such a view naturally coheres with the idea that the person of Jesus brings peace to the animal world. Jesus' injunction is clear: "Go in peace and hurt no one; neither let any man injure you. . . ." The significance of the story consists not just in Jesus' filial relationships with animals, but specifically in how Jesus' presence realizes in time that original vision of peaceful co-existence that God willed from the beginning. Because of their sinlessness, animals are able to prefigure, and respond to, the presence of Jesus, which joyfully returns creation to its original state of paradisal innocence. The theology behind this story then is truly biblical and orthodox, even though it may be the work of embellishment and imagination. The writer makes explicit those themes of kinship and peacefulness that are only implicit in the canonical Gospels. And the telling thing is that the popularity of this Gospel kept alive a more inclusive, animal-friendly vision of peaceableness and redemption at a time when the very notion that there could be friendship with animals was being derided by, for example, scholastic theologians like St. Thomas Aquinas. As I suggest elsewhere,[18] the lives of saints and St. Francis of Assisi in particular represent an alternative tradition to that of scholastic theologians.

Overall, what these texts demonstrate is that interest in and concern for animals remained a theme of Christian thinking and imagining during the first centuries of Church history. Contrary to many commentators, these texts do contain insights of considerable theological value. It really is not good enough for scholars, like William Morrice, just to dismiss for example the Infancy Gospels as possessing "little historical or theological value."[19] Quite what their historical value is, is currently undeterminable, at least precisely. Some may be entirely legendary. Some may comprise genuine historical reminiscence. Some may yet turn out to constitute vital sources of illumination in understanding the complex three or four centuries of Christian history following the death of Jesus. I am inclined to a much more positive (and I hope more open) evaluation of their historical value. But historical value apart, their theological value, especially at a time when ethical discussion about our treatment of animals is increasingly topical, should not be underestimated.

It is often supposed that Christian thought has been indifferent or hostile to animals, and there is a great deal of evidence to support that view. But these (and many other) texts are testimony to an abiding interest by Christians of various persuasions and at various times, spanning a significant period of early Church history. And a great deal of this concern and reflection has been—in comparison with many ages including our own—remarkably positive and ethically enlightened. One recent commentator has written that "we may assume that the basic underlying message of the speaking animal narratives calls on the hearer to display, at least, the dignity and sensitivity to the divine displayed by these animals," and that readers are being asked to affirm "that there is no life, be it human or animal, apart from God."[20] Understanding that sense of relatedness, even of communion and fellowship, is a strand of spiritual reflection that still awaits theological recognition and ethical realization.

Animals and Vegetarianism in Early Chinese Christianity

In 2004, Professor Mang Ping of the China University of Poli-
tics and Law Press asked me if I would be prepared to allow
my Animal Gospel *to be published in Chinese. Of course, I*
jumped at the opportunity and offered to write a new Preface
specifically for Chinese readers. For months, I pondered how I
could commend Christian concern for animals to an entirely
new readership to whom notions of animal rights might appear
rather foreign. I need not have worried. In the course of my
research, I discovered that the Chinese had been there before
the rest of us, and already had a distinguished and remarkable
tradition of reverence for life. This is but one example of many
voices and movements of compassion for animals that have
been silenced or marginalized. The Preface was published in
the Chinese edition in 2005 of Animal Gospel, *and an English*
language version in Madang, *4 (December 2005).* Madang *is*
the International Journal of Contextual Theology *in East Asia*
and published by the Korean Association of Progressive Theolo-
gians. What follows is a revised version of the journal article.

I

During the last thirty years, there have been intense philosophical debates about how we should treat animals and specifically about the concept of "animal rights." At first sight, this
concern for animals might appear a Western import, perhaps
even a concession to modern, predominantly secular Western thinking that is sometimes unfavorably characterized as

suffering from a surfeit of sentimentality about animals. This reaction, however understandable, is seriously mistaken.

Consider: in the ancient Confucian temple of Xian, there is a stone stele, originally erected in AD 781, and known, tendentiously or unhelpfully, as the Nestorian Stone. It tells the story of an ancient religion called "the Religion of Light," led by a monk called Aluoben, who first visited China during the Tang Dynasty. It describes how, when the Emperor heard its new teaching, he was struck by its "mysterious and wonderful" quality, and allowed Aluoben to establish a monastery in the Da Qin province.

The Stone offers this description of the new religion: "To penetrate the mysteries, to bless with a good conscience, to be great yet empty, to return to stillness and be forgiving, to be compassionate . . . to help them understand the nature of things, to maintain purity, to nourish all things, to respect all life, and to answer the needs of those whose beliefs come from the heart—these are the services the Religion of Light Church can offer." At first sight, these aspirations might appear largely Buddhist or Taoist, yet the Stone continues:

> The True Lord of the Primordial Void, in absolute stillness and constant naturalness, crafted and nourished all things. He raised the earth and established the sky. He *took on human form and His compassion was limitless.* The sun rises; darkness is banished; and we are witnesses to the true wonder.[1]

The reference to the "True Lord . . . taking human form" is so unmistakably Christian that it is difficult not to conclude that this "Religion of Light" was Christian in origin, and that monk Aluoben and his followers were none other than early Christian missionaries.

Consider further: in the Da Qin province, where the monks first settled, can be found a pagoda that dates back to the seventh century and which, remarkably, bears the marks of early Christian worship. Excavated in 1999 with the support of the Chinese Government, the second floor of the pagoda shows the remains of an eighth- to ninth-century sculpture of the nativity with the Virgin Mary in a reclining position, as sometimes depicted in Russian icons of that period. Unusually, the central court of the pagoda runs from east to west (as do all Christian churches) unlike Buddhist or Taoist temples, which characteristically run from north to south.

Consider yet further: at the now famous caves in Dunhuang, many ancient manuscripts were discovered during the first decades of the twentieth century and, sad to say, largely looted by Westerners and sold to private collectors. Among the Buddhist and Taoist manuscripts were some apparently Christian ones, later described as "the Jesus Sutras." The Second Sutra—the Sutra of the World Honored One—tells us that it was written "after the physical manifestation took place [i.e. Christ's birth] 641 years ago,"[2] which dates the manuscript closely to the visit of Aluoben in the seventh century. The same Sutra echoes the familiar Gospel idea that God cares even for sparrows, and the second Sutra—the Sutra of Cause and Effect and Salvation—speaks of how the "One Sacred Spirit looks with compassion on all life."[3]

In the Fourth Sutra—the Sutra of Jesus Christ—the fifth "covenant" or commandment requires that "any living being should not only not take the life of another living being, but should also teach others to do likewise." Again, elsewhere, "God protects all that lives: everything that lives does so as a result of this. It is forbidden to take a life even for sacrifice, for these teachings forbid taking any life."[4] John the Baptist is described as a vegetarian: one "who dwelt in the wilderness and who, from his birth, had never eaten meat or drunk wine, but instead lived on vegetables and honey gathered from the wilderness."[5] The meaning of Jesus' death is described in universal terms: "The Messiah gave up his body to the wicked ones for the sake of all living beings. . . . In his compassion he gave up his life." And, remarkably, the day before the resurrection, when Jesus hung upon the Cross, is described as the "sixth cleansing, *vegetarian* day."[6]

For this narrative, and the translations of the Jesus Sutras, I am indebted to the pioneering work of Sinologist Martin Palmer.[7] His work makes remarkable reading. If Palmer is right (and I have no reason to doubt his evidence), there existed in China an early Christian Church whose "teachings on charity, vegetarianism, anti-slavery, equality of men and women, and care for nature . . . offer models of personal behaviour that draw on the best in Christianity and in other ancient spiritual traditions."[8]

II

Many questions crowd in. Who was Aluoben? Was he a monk, or actually a bishop, sent (possibly) by the Syrian or Persian churches? Why do we apparently have no other records of him? Why would Aluoben and his followers have been given such special treatment by an Emperor not usually known for his non-violent convictions? What were the precise doctrinal beliefs of the church, and how extensive were its contacts with Taoism and Buddhism? And how many other "Jesus Sutras" might there be, hidden in private collections, which could yet spread further light on the phenomenon of early Chinese Christianity?

Many of these questions are not yet susceptible to anything like complete answers. But unless the research is utterly tendentious (which I doubt), it does seem indisputable that there existed an authentic Christian Church in China long before the Jesuit missionaries arrived in the late sixteenth century. And, what is more, this Christian community was committed to a doctrine of non-violence to animals as well as humans, lived a vegetarian life, and preached a Gospel of compassion for all living beings.

Some scholars might argue that the "Religion of Light" was obviously a syncretistic faith, which borrowed freely from Taoism and Buddhism, and this in turn explains its apparent concern for the compassionate treatment of animals. That there is some Buddhist and Taoist influence in the Sutras is undeniable. Just a few examples will suffice. The reference to "karma" and the "five *skhandas*" in the Second Sutra are explicable in relation to Buddhist sutras, though even here, despite the formal similarity, the point behind the reference to "karma" is an explanation of what it means to be saved "from"—presumably in a context in which the notion of "sin" was not easily comprehensible. Elsewhere in the Fourth Sutra there is a reference to the Buddhas (semi-divine beings) who orbit the Messiah, and also the acknowledgment that there are "great teachers, such as the Buddhas" but, in context, such teachers are understood to be "moved by the Wind" (which appears to be a reference to God the Spirit), and are clearly subordinate to this power.[9]

It would be astonishing, of course, if early Christianity learned nothing from its cultural setting in China, as it has learned and borrowed from its development in other contexts, whether they be Greek, Roman or Syrian. All preaching of the Christian message is radically influenced—necessarily so—by its environment. What can be understood obviously determines what is said. The real question is: was the development of what may be loosely called "Taoist Christianity" a legitimate one?

In fact, what is remarkable about the Sutras is the way in which, despite a vastly different cultural setting, they maintain strongly orthodox theological leanings, and indicate a process of theological development. The case of animals illustrates this. The First Sutra says:

> Watch the birds: they don't plant or harvest, and they have no houses to worry about. They do no work, yet are fed and watered and never worry about what to wear, because [of] the One who cares for them. You are more important than birds, so why do you worry?[10]

These words are obviously based on St. Matthew's Gospel 6:25–26, or on an oral or written tradition known to both. They reflect entirely accurately the spirit of Matthew's recorded saying of Jesus, which concerns God's providential care as Creator of all. The Second Sutra, possibly under Taoist influence, speaks of how "The One Sacred Spirit made a vast multitude of beings. Everything under Heaven is filled with this Sacred Space,"[11] and goes on to describe the various qualities of the individual soul. The Third Sutra repeats this point, but elaborates: "All that exists does so as the manifestation of the beingness of the One Sacred Spirit."[12] And the

Fourth Sutra describes Jesus as the embodiment of compassion for all living beings.

These are entirely orthodox reflections, albeit influenced by other cultural thought forms. The starting point is that God as Creator cares for all living beings, his Spirit enables other God-given breathing lives, which are therefore manifestations of the same divine Spirit, and finally, Jesus as Messiah expresses the sovereign care of the Creator by dying for the redemption of all creatures from earthly suffering. The Sutras make explicit what is actually already implicit in canonical scripture, for example in the Prologue to St. John's Gospel, and in St. Paul's letter to the Romans, where he speaks of suffering creation awaiting its deliverance from "bondage to decay" (Romans 8:18–24, RSV).

III

Some may argue that, even if this is so, the emphasis on vegetarianism is surely Buddhist rather than Christian. Even that claim bears some examination. Like most theologians, I have assumed, in accordance with the canonical Gospels, that Jesus ate fish, and possibly (but not certainly) meat. But that view needs to be balanced by three other considerations, which raise some difficult (perhaps unanswerable) questions.

The first is the existence of an early Gospel called the Gospel of the Ebionites. We know that it existed because it is attacked as "heretical" by Epiphanius, the fourth-century Bishop of Salamis, in his principal work *Panarion*, which lists and condemns various heresies. The Ebionites were, it seems, a Jewish-Christian sect whose written Gospel was regarded by Epiphanius as a distortion of the Aramaic Gospel of Matthew. His attack refers to some of the actual lines of their Gospel:

> And it came to pass when John was baptised, that the Pharisees came to him and were baptised, and all Jerusalem also. He had a garment of camel's hair, and a leathern girdle about his loins. And his meat was wild honey, which tasted like manna, formed like cakes of oil.

They say [the Ebionites] that he [Jesus] is not begotten by the Father but created like one of the archangels, being greater than they. He rules over the angels and the beings created by God and he came and declared, as the gospel used by them records: "I have come to abolish the sacrifices: if you do not cease from sacrificing, the wrath [of God] will not cease from weighing upon you."

Those who reject meat have inconsiderably fallen into error and said, "I have no desire to eat the flesh of this Paschal Lamb with you." They leave the true order of the words and distort the word which is clear to all from the connection of the words and make the disciples say: "Where do you want us to prepare for you to eat the Passover?" To which he [Jesus] replied, "I have no desire to eat the flesh of the Paschal Lamb with you."[13]

We do not know whether Epiphanius represents the Gospel of the Ebionites fairly or accurately, but we may be struck by the apparent similarity between the depiction of John the Baptist as a vegetarian and also the rejection of animal sacrifices in both the Ebionite Gospel and the Jesus Sutras. (The rejection of the idea that Jesus ate the Paschal Lamb also seems to resonate with the otherwise inexplicable idea in the Sutras that the last day of crucifixion was a "vegetarian day" or, alternatively, it may be due to reflection on the sixth day of creation as depicted in Genesis 1:29–30 where God decrees a vegetarian diet.) This raises the question of whether the Gospel of the Ebionites is actually a source for the Jesus Sutras, or whether both are utilizing a common written or oral source, which may have had wide provenance in the ancient Eastern world. Some, like Keith Akers, have argued that this original community of Jewish-Christians faithfully recorded the witness of Jesus to a non-violent way of life (inclusive of animals) marked by a special concern for the poor (hence their name "Ebionite," derived from the Hebrew term EBIONIM meaning "the poor" Christians).[14]

The second consideration is allied to the first. From the existence of the Ebionite Gospel, we know that vegetarian Christians existed until a long period after Jesus' death. The Ebionite

Gospel was probably (but not certainly) written at the beginning of the second century AD. From Epiphanius's attack sometime in the fourth century we may assume that an Ebionite community had existed for a considerable time, and may still have been active in his lifetime. The question should therefore be raised as to why there were *any* Christian vegetarians at all, if their grounds for vegetarianism could be so easily rebutted by those who could give contrary testimony—even by those who may have been living witnesses to Jesus' own meat-eating.

In fact, we know that Christian vegetarians existed right from the beginning because St. Paul also attacks them in his letter (around AD 60) to the Roman Church. He writes: "As for the man who is weak in faith, welcome him, but not for disputes over opinions. One believes he may eat anything, while the weak man eats only vegetables" (Romans 14:1–2, RSV). The apparent cause of the disagreement concerned the propriety of eating meat offered in sacrifices to idols, but although the controversy took this precise form, it is possible that it hid a deeper disagreement about the propriety of eating meat in the first place. Although St. Paul regards the issue as simply one of "conscience," he nowhere explicitly states what one would have expected him to say, namely that since our Lord ate meat, there should be no problem about his followers doing so. But if Jesus ate meat, possibly meat offered to "idols," even (according to one scholar) sacrificing animals himself,[15] why should there be any Christian vegetarians at all, let alone some to whom Paul is prepared to make concessions of "conscience"?

The third consideration arises from the apparent fact that James, the brother of Jesus, was a vegetarian. This raises the obvious question about Jesus' family history. It is unclear whether the references in the tradition to the vegetarianism of James are due to ascetical or moral objections, or a combination of both. But one recent scholar, Robert Eisenman, in an exhaustive study, relates the issue back to the Noahic covenant, which suggests that James adopted a form of theologically inspired vegetarianism, which had an ethical dimension.[16] Given that there were Christian vegetarians who apparently appealed to Jesus himself as their authority, the question arises as to the nature of their vegetarianism and how it was understood. Was it simply a cultic, ascetical rejection or was it based on some rejection of the morality of killing animals for food?

Some scholars have been eager to view vegetarianism as an expression of ascetical rather than moral concern. Roger T. Beckwith describes the vegetarian practice of the Therapeutae as the "vegetarianism of the ascetics." While the Therapeutae were (as far as we know) first-century monastics and therefore generally ascetic in character, their desire to keep their table "pure from the flesh of animals" (as Philo remarks) seems to owe its origin to the Old Testament prohibition against eating blood. It was therefore, as Beckwith acknowledges, a theologically inspired vegetarianism, which led to a rejection of the Temple and the sacrificial system itself. But it is difficult to think that this so-called "spiritualisation of the sacrificial law" had absolutely no moral content.[17] When one combines this with the decree of the Jerusalem Council in Acts 15:20 regarding abstinence from "what is strangled with blood" (who else is "strangled" but animals for food rather than sacrifice?), one begins to wonder whether there are deep-seated motifs at play here of which we are only partly or dimly aware. At any rate, it is worth reflecting on the simple known fact that there were theologically inspired Christian vegetarians at a very early point in the Church's life.

These considerations do not, of course, close the issue of whether Jesus was a vegetarian. There is serious evidence on the other side, most notably Jesus' fish eating and his apparent breaking down of food restrictions (Mark 7:19). The debate is still open and it is unwise to be dogmatic. But it is possible, and at least *thinkable*, that early Jewish-Christian groups have faithfully preserved Jesus' example of vegetarianism and his objection to animal sacrifice, and that is the same tradition that the Ebionites represent in their Gospel, and that in turn is reflected in the Jesus Sutras. Scholars have yet to wrestle with the implications of the fact that there was an early sub-tradition of Christian vegetarianism, which apparently claimed dominical or canonical authority.

In short, then, while we may be tempted to view the Sutras as reflections of contemporary Buddhist thought or practice, it is by no means clear that this is actually the case. It is possible that contact with Buddhism reinforced, rather than originated, an ethical concern for other living creatures. It would not be the first time that a religious tradition's creative encounter with another has re-activated authentic elements within its own.

IV

It will be seen that the debate about animals—how we should live with them and how we should treat them—is by no means a modern one, least of all a purely secular one. Rather, it is a deep spiritual issue that emerges within many world religious traditions; unsurprisingly, perhaps, there is also a similar debate in Buddhism about whether the Buddha himself was vegetarian, and whether all Buddhists should be vegetarian today.[18]

Whether we are Christians, Buddhists, Taoists, or of no faith, it is difficult to speak meaningfully of compassion without also extending that notion to our treatment other creatures capable of suffering pain. If Taoists and Buddhists have helped Christians to re-discover something essential to their faith then Christians should be truly thankful. The generous God—or "the Sacred Spirit"—is not confined within human thoughts or human traditions, however well intentioned or noble.

The Taoist Church lasted, it seems, until the collapse of the Tang Dynasty in 906 or 907. It subsequently suffered such persecution that the Da Qin monastery—and many others—were completely destroyed, and only the Stone and the (now restored) pagoda remain as visible symbols of the world these early Christians sought to create. But there are still believers, like myself, who are eager to see the rebirth of an authentic non-violent and compassionate Christian faith.[19] In fact, Chinese and Asian Christians have an opportunity—perhaps a unique one in world Christianity—to engage thoughtfully and constructively with the new movements of ethical sensitivity for the environment, vegetarianism, and animal protection, and to demonstrate how these emerging concerns resonate with the deepest aspirations of authentic Asian Christianity.

On Being an Animal Liturgist

This essay is more personal than the rest. It tells the story that led to my writing the controversial book Animal Rites: Liturgies of Animal Care in 1999. It also explains the theological and pastoral motivation behind the book and describes some of the reactions. Despite the controversy, there is growing evidence of a liturgical movement for animals that now includes hundreds of animal blessings or animal welfare services every year. Segments of the essay are to be found in my article on "Animal Burials" in the as-yet-unpublished Andrew Linzey (ed.), The Encyclopaedia of Global Animal Concern and in an article I wrote on animal blessing services for the Church Times on 1 October 2004. An abridged and revised version also appeared in The Way, a Jesuit Journal of contemporary spirituality, 46/4 (October 2006).

Barney was a refugee. Abandoned, he subsequently found a home at the local animal sanctuary. It was there that we first met him. His shaggy hair, dark brown eyes, and exuberant temperament endeared him to the Linzey family. "There goes the wooly rocket," we would say as he raced before us on long walks. So glad was he to have a home that when any of us opened the front door he would pin us to the wall and lavish his affection upon us. He had, I recall, very large paws. He made ample use of them when he wanted our attention. Still, he gave us much more than we gave him.

Diagnosed with some neurological problem, he suddenly went into seizures and never recovered. Euthanasia was the advised course of action. The result was devastating for the whole family. Here was a dog badly treated by the world, who we could not even save from suffering and premature death. We elected to bury him in the garden. As we stood around the open grave, I fumbled to find some appropriate words of parting.

But there were no prescribed words. The physical neglect that Barney had suffered was paralleled by a spiritual neglect. The churches had really nothing to offer—and nothing to say. Christians inherit two thousand years of spirituality and scholarship, and yet are silent—at least liturgically—about the deaths of millions of other species, even those who share and enrich our lives. A tradition that has countenanced the blessing of cars and houses has never even registered a pastoral need in relation to the death of companion animals.

Struck by this lacuna, I was determined to do something. I phoned up my publishers and said that I wanted a break from my publishing commitments to complete a book on animal liturgy. They obliged with a contract. "Should only take a month or so," I foolishly commented. In fact, it took as long as six and consumed a whole summer. It was an agonizing process. All very flattering to be thought a pioneer but, in reality, I felt more like a scavenger in a wasteland. Some of my friends judged the project distinctly eccentric.

What was the problem then that I sought to address? Quite simply: the invisibility of animals in Christian worship. Christians currently worship God as though the world of animals does not exist. Contrary to some of the psalms, praise has become an exclusively humanocentric affair; animals hardly get a look in at all. Behind this is a deeper impoverishment, or rather blindness: the sense that God the Creator is not much concerned with animals either. If we neglect them, we simply follow the route laid out by traditional versions of divine negligence. But this view is increasingly impossible to sustain once it is really grasped that God is the Creator not only of the human species, but also of millions of species of life. Can the same God who nourishes and sustains the entire created universe really only be interested in *one* species? "An exclusive preoccupation with human well-being is beginning to seem distinctly parochial."[1]

Allied to that, is the question of the flesh. Anglican theology, it is sometimes boasted, has a strong incarnational tradition. If true, it is odd that many clergy and theologians still have not grasped the spiritual significance of our relations with other fleshly creatures. It is worth pausing to reflect why the most "fleshly" (at least in theory) religion of all has difficulty in celebrating animals, even recognizing them as subjects of moral solicitude.

The doctrine of the incarnation teaches us, at least theoretically, to take the flesh seriously. I used the following passage from Louis Bouyer in my Introduction to the book: "[Humanity] will thus come to realize that the originality of Christianity consists in consecrating their everyday lives through the Incarnation, and not in attempting to live in a world that is supposed to be holy but which is in fact artificial and out of contact with reality."[2] This everyday world, which is supposed to be consecrated by the incarnation, is populated with *other* creatures. "There is something distinctly odd, even perverse, about an incarnational theology that cannot celebrate our relations with other creatures," I groaned. Even more despairingly, "I am getting a little tired of theologians who are eager, sometimes over-eager, to see incarnational resonances within almost every area of human activity (visual art, music, poetry, dance) but who look with astonishment that our relations with animals might be an issue worthy of spiritual, nay incarnational, concern."[3]

Christian theology is still deeply threatened by talk of animals, as if by taking their interests seriously we dethrone our own. Indeed one theologian was recently foolish enough to state his fear dogmatically: "The root of the case for animal rights lies there. Its advocates do not believe that [humanity] is unique."[4] But this fear-projecting theologian clearly had not read my works that defend both animal rights and human uniqueness.[5] For some people, some things cannot be true no matter how much evidence to the contrary. Perhaps some Christians are simply frightened of displays of emotion toward animals. Some clergy, I know, look askance at celebrations of inter-species fraternity, arguing that they pander to sentimentality. "People love animals," says Geraldine Granger, the TV

Vicar of Dibley, justifying her intention to hold an animal service. "People also love food mixers," replies the straight-laced churchwarden, David Horton. "But there are very few of us pressing the Archbishop of Canterbury for a special communion for the Moulinex Magic-Master."[6]

But there are obvious differences between food mixers and animals. The chief one is that animals are God's creatures. That's an obvious point, but behind it lie weighty theological insights. Animals were created alongside us, according to Genesis 1, on the sixth day of creation. They are blessed by their Creator. They are given their own space to live and flourish. Their life, *nephesh*, is God-given. The God who creates also enters into a covenant relationship with all living beings. Given these insights, it is only appropriate that individuals should experience a sense of fellow-feeling with other sentient species. And this is most keenly felt by people who care for them, and keep them as companions. Some animal services, I accept, can make their prime focus little more than a celebration of childish emotion. But, as I get older, I am less censorious about "childish emotion." Vincent van Gogh once remarked that in order to love God one needs to love "many things":

> Love a friend, a wife, something, whatever you like, and you will be on the right way to know more about it. . . . But one must love with a lofty and serious intimate sympathy, with strength, with intelligence and one must always try to know deeper, better, and more. That leads to God, that leads to unwavering faith.[7]

The bottom line is that lots of people love their animals and dare to think that God does too.

When people speak of "sentimentality," what they often have in mind is that certain emotional responses are inappropriate, and some may be. It is reinforced by the rather straight-laced line in the *Catechism of the Catholic Church*: "One can love animals; one should not direct to them the affection due only to persons."[8] That almost suggests that there is only a limited amount of love in the world so we should not waste it on animals. How can it be reconciled, one wonders, with the extraordinary love of other creatures displayed by many Catholic saints? Can the emotional rationing proposed coexist with Christ-like generosity?

But emotional response, even if it is worthy as a starter, is not enough. There are big theological questions that should be addressed. Although clergy are often reticent about giving them voice, many "ordinary" worshippers have grasped them: If God loves and cares for creation, should not the species uniquely made in God's image also demonstrate that same loving care? If our power over animals is not to be its own self-justification, should not the example of moral generosity—of lordship expressed in service—glimpsed in the life and example of Jesus be the model for the exercise of our own "dominion" over other creatures? Far from creation being "made for us," is it not truer, and more adequately biblical, to say that humans are made for creation—to act as servants and guardians of what God has created? Animal services can, at best, provide a platform to say important theological things about animals. These include the need for a sense of wonder and awe at divine creativity, an appreciation that God delights in differentiated being, and that we should delight in it too, and, not least of all, a penitential recognition of human hubris and greed that results in animal abuse.

There are also many, largely un-met, spiritual needs. People who keep animals have often made an elementary but profound discovery: animals are not machines or commodities, but beings with their own God-given lives, individuality, and personality. At their best, relations with companion animals can help us to grow in mutuality, self-giving, and trust. And yet, these spiritually sustaining relationships often go unrecognized. For many, animals are the "significant others" in their lives. Indeed, one recent theologian has suggested that in these relationships of apparent "excess" we see nothing less than the self-giving of God. "I want to suggest that, from a theological perspective that takes pets seriously," writes Stephen H. Webb, "animals are more like gifts than something owned, giving us more than we expect and thus obliging us to return their gifts."[9] Far from decrying these relationships as "sentimental," "unbalanced," or "obsessive," as frequently happens today, churches could point to their underlying theological significance as examples of divine grace.

Some view liturgical concern for animals as a sell-out to a post-modernist, largely secular sensibility. In fact, blessings for animals are found in the Catholic manual, *Rituale Romanum*, first written in 1614, and virtually left untouched until 1952. Moreover, as we have seen, concern for animals as a Christian duty was pioneered by the SPCA (as it then was), whose first Prospectus even proposed the funding of "periodic discourses" from London pulpits.[10] Many clergy have not caught up with the fact that modern ethical sensibility to animals was largely Christian in origin.

Anyhow, I busied my summer away determined to find the words the Christian tradition had not said but which (I thought) it always really deep down wanted to say, yet somehow did not find the time or effort to do so. I began, unsurprisingly, with a liturgy for animal burials. What should one say when confronted, as I was, with a dead dog and a hole in the ground? I came to the conclusion that what we should want to say at that poignant moment is very similar to what one already says, and does, when a human being dies. One should first pray a prayer of thanksgiving, and then commend the life of the individual concerned into the hands of Almighty God. I wrestled in my own mind with the theology of hope and came even more firmly to the conclusion expressed without dissent at the Anglican Church's Lambeth Conference of 1998 that "the redemptive purpose of God in Jesus Christ extends to the whole of creation."[11] The God of the universe could find space even, and especially, for Barney. Immodestly, I felt pleased with at least some of my efforts, this one especially:

> Pilgrim God
> who journeys with us
> through the joys and shadows
> of this world
> be with us
> in our sorrow
> and feel our pain;

help us to accept
the mystery of death
without bitterness
but with hope.
Among the shadows
of this world,
amid the turmoil of life
and the fear of death
you stand alongside us,
always blessing, always giving
arms always outstretched.
For this we know:
every living thing is yours
and returns to you.
As we ponder this mystery
we give you thanks
for the life of (Name)
and we now commit *him/her*
into your loving hands.
Gentle God:
fragile is your world,
delicate are your creatures,
and costly is your love
which bears and redeems us all.
Amen.[12]

Some people may cavil at the confident notion that animals are redeemed *individually*.[13] Even among those who believe in animal redemption, there are some who do not believe that animals have the right "soul" for immortality. Catholic tradition has distinguished between the "rational" soul that equips humans for eternity and the "non-rational" soul of animals who perish after death. But that absolute emphasis on rationality (at least as we understand it) seems inappropriate when we are talking of divine grace. Simply put, it misses the point. And the point concerns *God's* benevolence, not ours. I cannot with certainty look into an animal's psyche and register a conclusion about its spiritual status, but I can be sure—as sure as I am of anything—that the merciful God disclosed in Jesus

Christ will not let any loved creature perish into oblivion. To deny this Gospel of hope to all other species except our own strikes me as an arrogantly mean doctrine of God.

In fact, the idea of cosmic redemption (and, by implication, individuals within it) is hardly new. The Logos doctrine, so prevalent during the early years of Christian history, encapsulates (forgive the pun) it all. Indeed, Allan Galloway, in his classic work *The Cosmic Christ*, argues that the doctrine of cosmic redemption "was at the very heart of the primitive Gospel."[14] Developing precisely that theme, my words of commendation were prefaced by a robust theology of the Logos:

> Christ is the first and the last,
> the Alpha and Omega
> who reconciles and redeems
> every form of created life;
> the source and destiny
> of all living things;
> who bears the wounds
> of all suffering creatures;
> who transforms all
> suffering into joy;
> Christ is the first and the last
> the Alpha and the Omega;
> the Saviour of the Universe:
> in Christ shall all be made alive.[15]

But the book did not only contain liturgies for animal burials. It also included services in celebration of animal companionship, services for animal welfare, healing liturgies, new eucharistic prayers "for the whole creation," and forms for the blessing of individual animals. Underlying all these attempts was the need to develop liturgy that helped us celebrate the God-given lives of other creatures. The following are some examples:

> God of the universe,
> all creatures praise you;
> the sun setting on the lake;

the birds flying upward toward the heavens;
the growl of the bear;
the darting of the stickleback;
the purring of the cat;
the wide eyes of the tiger;
the swift legs of the cheetah;
the dance of the hare;
the lapping of the dog;
the descent of the dove.
God of a thousand ears
the music of your creatures
resounds throughout creation
and in heaven a symphony is made.
Christ in all things:
in the waves breaking on the shore;
in the beauty of the sunset;
in the fragrant blossom of Spring;
in the music that makes our hearts dance;
in the kisses of embracing love;
in the cries of the innocent.
Help us to wonder, Lord,
to stand in awe;
to stand and stare;
and so to praise you
for the richness of the world
you have laid before us.
Large and immense God,
help us to know the littleness
of our lives without you;
the littleness of our thoughts
without your inspiration;
and the littleness of our hearts
without your love;
you are God beyond our littleness
yet in one tiny space and time
you became one with us
and all those specks of dust
you love for all eternity;
enlarge our hearts and minds

to reverence all living things
and in our care for them
to become big with your grace
and signs of your kingdom. Amen.[16]

I expected that the book would arouse interest, but I was not prepared for the media roller coaster that followed. Scores of media outlets worldwide focused on the book, ranging from the *Washington Post*[17] and *Der Spiegel*[18] to the Dutch daily *Trouw*.[19] In addition, the *Independent* gave over almost a page to an extended interview.[20] I spent three weeks either on the phone talking to journalists or darting from one studio to another.

Two reactions predominated. The first was defensiveness. The opening shot was fired by the Church of England press office, which apparently informed journalists that the liturgies were "illegal." Since Church of England worship is governed by common as well as ecclesial law, the implication was doubly serious. Thankfully, the claim was unfounded since canon law allows clergy "discretion" in the use of liturgies other than those formally prescribed by the General Synod. But that such a charge should be made at all was a sign of official defensiveness. Church spokesperson Arun Kataria commented: "A priest may use alternative forms of worship but 'must be satisfied that his bishop will not feel [the priest] in any way had done anything irreverent or unseemly.'"[21] That implied that I was about to do something indecent. I wonder if the same strictures apply to clergy who bless foxhunts and whaling ships.

The *Church Times* sought out theological adversaries, but found them oddly mute. "Teachers of ethics at two theological colleges I approached refused to comment or be quoted, because they had 'nothing to say,'" reported the journalist. Quite what produced such a mute condition, I cannot tell. However,

A brother of the Society of St. Francis at its house in Hilfield, who preferred not to be named, [commented], "We like animals. We have several ourselves. But our main interest is in people. Animals were peripheral to St. Francis, which many people don't realise. He was more concerned about people."[22]

The idea that St. Francis could be concerned about *both* humans and animals—as could modern-day Franciscans—was obviously a thought that eluded him. More seriously, it was a bit disconcerting to discover that a Franciscan brother really had not grasped that the Gospel that St. Francis preached was about the love of God the Creator, which sustains all living beings—not just the human ones. Fortunately, some time later, I was invited to contribute to a Franciscan volume in which I was able to develop just this point:

> The theological significance behind the stories of St. Francis and the animals consists mainly in this: as we grow in union with, and love for, God the Creator, so we should likewise grow in communion with, and love of, God's other creatures. Far from being some kind of aberration, or distortion of the Gospel, concern for animals is a sign of true spirituality. If we wish to honor God the Creator, so we should honor fellow creatures.[23]

When approached for comment, Catholic theologians were not lost for words. The *Irish Independent* reported Michael Drumm, Head of the Mater Dei Institute in Dublin, as saying that the book was "offensive" because "Baptism and funeral rituals are entwined with human faith. To use the same rituals for animals is demeaning," he declared.[24] But since the book did not contain any baptismal liturgies, it was a classic example of a media set-up. In the same vein, the editor of the *Irish Catholic*, David Quinn, reportedly "dismiss[ed]" the book, maintaining that "Most Catholics would find liturgies specifically attributed to animals as a ridiculous piece of sentimentality." And he added: "We have a duty not to be cruel to animals, but the idea of animals having souls bears more relation to Hinduism than Christianity."[25] In fact, Catholic theology has never denied that animals have souls—only rational and therefore immortal souls—but in the rush to judgment such distinctions were obviously not uppermost in his mind.

Not all Catholic reaction was uniformly hostile. *The Tablet* managed a fairly serious news announcement,[26] and the liturgical journal of the Catholic Bishops' Conference of

England and Wales managed some mollifying comments: "These prayers are serious and carefully compiled. There is much merit in them as regards liturgical structure and general style. They are not maudlin or sentimental." Pretty amazing, I thought. Then came the final paragraph:

> But is there any justification for incorporating specific animal liturgies in our worship? Animals may well have souls, but they are not immortal souls, and animals are not part of the salvific and sacramental economy in which humans are incorporated. Matthew 6:26 and 12:12 makes it clear that God cares for animals, but he values humans much more. Regretfully we must conclude that most of Professor Linzey's interesting liturgical texts are misconceived and inappropriate. They would assuredly not get past the Congregation for Divine Worship![27]

It is not that the texts did not get their approval that is vexing (that would have been too much to expect), but the theological reasons stated. Not "part of the salvific or sacramental economy" sounds weighty until one pauses to reflect that the Logos is the origin and destiny of all creaturely things, as many patristic writers have affirmed. How can animals not be part of the salvific economy if the Logos is the source of all life, as John's Gospel makes clear: "In him was life" (1:4)? What sense does it make to affirm God as the Creator of all but the redeemer of only the human species? Even the *Catechism of the Catholic Church* affirms unambiguously that the "world was created for the glory of God," and that "The ultimate purpose of creation is that God, who is creator of all things may at last become "all in all", thus simultaneously assuring his own glory and our beatitude."[28] "All in all" strikes me as difficult to reconcile with any "economy of salvation."

Moreover, it is a great mistake to make an absolute differentiation between human salvation and the salvation of creation. Of course, there are differences between animal and human redemption (humans, for example, need salvation because they are obviously sinful in a way in which animals cannot be), but it is the same creaturely "stuff" that is redeemed. To fail to see that is to fail to see the importance of the doctrine of Christ as the enfleshed Logos—a point well developed by C. N. Cochrane, who argues that the early Church claimed to possess in the Logos "a principle of understanding superior to anything existing in the classical world." Therefore, "To accept this faith was to believe that, however obscure this might appear to the scientific intelligence, the *esse* of the Father *embraced within itself* the elements of order and movement *and that these were not less integral than substance to the divine nature*. It was, moreover, to hold that on these essential constituents of the Deity *depended the structure and purpose of the universe*."[29] Less abstractly, the Logos is the taking of creaturely, fleshly stuff into the very nature of Godhead. All creation is saved through the Logos or there is no salvation. In short: the proposed reviewer's Catholic doctrine does not strike me as catholic enough, and in more than one sense.

The second reaction was ridicule. To some the whole idea of liturgically sanctioned concern for animals was something akin to a divine joke. That well-known and respected writer, A. N. Wilson, offered one of the more subtle (and therefore especially devastating) satires:

> We've been agonizing for some time about whether to have Percy baptised. It is difficult to subscribe to the old orthodoxies. On the other hand, if no one in future gets baptised, the church will die out. Do we really want Chartres Cathedral and the parish churches of England to become mere museums? And then there is the question of Percy himself. While I might feel shy about saying the creed, how can I know what is passing through his little head?
>
> It is a relief to discover, then, that the Rev Professor Andrew Linzey of Oxford University has published a series of "Animal Rites." There is not, as it happens, a form of Baptism for Dogs. For that, one would have to turn to Firbank's immortal *Eccentricities of Cardinal Pirelli*. But there is a form of Swearing a Covenant with a Companion Animal. . . . Such a ceremony would definitely help me to be more tolerant of the little fellow, a dog whose flatulence, halitosis and insatiable greed sometimes make him a difficult life-companion. . . . I shall remember it when Percy howls in the middle of *University Challenge*

[*College Bowl*—ed.] for no obvious reason. Professor Linzey has done much to correct the absurd anthropocentric view of the world which has formed so much Christian theology.[30]

More vexing was a feature in the *Mail on Sunday*, which, in the context of a serious interview, carried pictures of dressed up dogs apparently being prepared for a wedding service.[31] Although I had made absolutely clear that I was not in the business of canine weddings (or animal weddings of any sort), that maladroit impression was there for those who read no further than the sub-heading. One leading huntswoman subsequently accused me on radio of believing that animals should be married—it was, I think, a welcome digression from having to confront the issue in hand, namely cruelty to wild animals. Among the many other inanities, one German TV reporter fiercely questioned how one could bless a dog without also blessing its fleas. I confess I cannot recall, at that critical juncture, being able to give a theologically coherent response!

The Independent continued to find the story of interest. Another item appeared, this time in the newspaper's "Pandora" column:

Professor Andrew Linzey, holder of the world's first academic post in theology and animal welfare, at Mansfield College, Oxford, has had an unwelcome encounter with a dog. Linzey, who outraged church traditionalists by penning liturgies for animals, was bitten by a resident at Battersea Dogs' Home while filming a program for the BBC. Nowhere in his book, *Animal Rites*, does it say anything about prayers for animals who bite others. Has the dog-lover missed a trick? "I think some things are worth discussing, but not others," Linzey dryly told Pandora.[32]

In fact, I had not even spoken to Pandora, but there's no point in letting truth get in the way of a good joke.

There were, however, some thoughtful and interesting reviews. The *Expository Times* described me as a "pioneer" and argued that "one of the undeniable strengths of his work is that there is nothing of pantheism or new-ageism about it.

It endeavours to stand firmly within the Christian tradition, to reclaim that which, in his view has been lost or overlaid, and to reflect the concern of the Triune God for all of God's creation."[33] *Crucible*, the journal of the Board for Social Responsibility of the Church of England, praised me for providing "a welcome example of rebalancing a Christianity that has become too narrowly focused on human salvation rather than wrestling with the deeper belief that the whole of Creation is to be redeemed through Christ."[34] And it was gratifying when the Archbishop of Wales, Dr. Alwyn Rice Jones, endorsed the book as "a very necessary provision to help clergy and ministers to understand and appreciate the theme of Christian responsibility for creation."[35]

All in all, it was clear that the book had touched a nerve. This was evidenced by the scores of letters and phone calls from those who had recently been bereaved, and who were struggling to make sense of their loss. Many of them were deeply heartened to find a priest who actually thought their situation merited concern, even sympathy. Some of the letters were in fact heart-wrenching. Despite the bruises, I was glad that I risked ridicule to be of some small help to those who felt pastorally abandoned. In addition, I was pleased that some had seen a connection (however garbled the reporting) between the Word made flesh and people's actual lives with other fleshly creatures.

Animal Rites was not my first foray into animal liturgy. Back in 1975, as a theological student, I wrote the first *Order of Service for Animal Welfare*—published as a booklet by the RSPCA. My fellow theological students were, of course, incredulous, and had difficulty concealing their mirth. The booklet, however, sold very well, and is now in its sixth revised edition.[36] Hundreds of clergy of all denominations now hold such services, not just in the UK, but also in continental Europe, and increasingly in the USA. Most happen on 4 October, which is World Day for Animals, also the birthday of St. Francis of Assisi, or on the nearest Sunday, now designated "Animal Welfare Sunday."

On a lighter note, ministering to God's other creatures may occasionally be hazardous. I remember my first attempt at

blessing an animal. At the altar rail, a man was clutching a
ferret. I tried to administer a heavenly benediction. "No, don't
touch it," he exclaimed, "it'll have yer ****ing fingers off."[37]
When, subsequently, I hear clergy speaking of how they "don't
touch" animal services, a smile comes to my face.

"But animals make a mess," it is objected. Whenever I hear
that, I am reminded of the view of Albert Schweitzer, who
likened the history of Western philosophy to that of a person who cleans the kitchen floor, only to find that the dog
comes in and muddies it with paw prints.[38] Animals do make a
mess of humanocentric theology. Despite some organizational
difficulties (usually very minor), the bringing of animals into
church has a deep symbolic importance—one that is seldom
lost on the human participants. It symbolizes the inclusion
of the animal world into the very place where so much theology has excluded them. It also provides a practical glimpse of
creation in praise.

And the noise? Well, what is a dirge to one person is bird
song to another. In fact, I am usually astonished at other creatures' sense of place, but when interactive barking takes place
(as it sometimes does), I remind my hearers that if St. Francis
of Assisi can preach to the birds, Andrew Linzey can be heck-
led by dogs.

Summing Up

Towards a Prophetic Church for Animals

If the last essay was the most personal, this one is the most challenging. In 2000, the Anglican Society for the Welfare of Animals (ASWA) held a Millennial Service for Animal Welfare at Southwark Cathedral. I was invited to give an address and I chose to examine—as realistically as possible—how far the Church of England could ever go in endorsing ethical concern for animals, and what would need to happen for it to move from its current state of indifference, if not negligence. Although I focus on my own Church, the proposed strategy is relevant to almost all Christian churches. The following is a revised version of the address previously published by ASWA as a booklet in 2000. Since it touches on many of the issues raised in the book, it serves as a summing up.

Since this is a service in an Anglican Cathedral, perhaps you will forgive me if I begin by addressing the situation in the Anglican Communion. When it comes to animals, I fear the Church of England needs a good talking to, and I don't intend to miss this opportunity. As we all know, the Church of England is the Church established by law. Its Supreme Governor is the Queen. The archbishops, bishops, provosts, and deans are appointed in practice by the Prime Minister—albeit with some input from the Church. Twenty-six bishops have seats in the House of Lords. Even Church worship is governed by law. The Church of England is the established Church, and in more than one sense.

The question must therefore be asked: Can this same Church, rooted in law, convention, and privilege, really speak for the poor, the weak, the vulnerable, the disadvantaged, and those on the margins of society? And, most fundamentally, can it speak on behalf of those that are the weakest and most vulnerable of all, namely God's other sentient creatures? I raise this question because there are agnostic friends of mine who view our aspirations as a lost cause. The Church of England, they say, can never really represent the cause of justice for animals because it is too compromised by its associations with the powerful, especially those who benefit from the exploitation of animals. We are, they say—if you will forgive the animal analogy—simply barking up the wrong tree.

And if the Church cannot even represent the human poor, the human dispossessed, and the human disadvantaged, what hope can animals have? To take one case in point, what hope can animals in laboratories have when the Church (or at least most of its ethical spokespeople) currently supports destructive experimentation on embryos, arguably the weakest humans of them all?

There are few signs that the Church really sees, let alone understands, the cause of animals. Yes, the Church understands well the needs of farmers, and the problems that beset the farming community, but does the Church really see the suffering of farm animals? Does it have any appreciation of what they have to endure in intensive farming—debeaking, castration, tail docking without anesthetics, battery cages—to take only a few examples? The Church grasps with an easygoing certainty the utilitarian arguments of scientific researchers, but does it equally comprehend the suffering that animals have to undergo in laboratories throughout the world? Where, I wonder, are the Christian protests at the dramatic rise in genetic experiments on animals? The Church is fully appreciative of the needs of industry and commerce, but does it also know the cost that animals have to pay when they are treated as economic commodities—when they are genetically manipulated, patented, reared in miserable conditions, exported abroad or over long distances only to await grisly slaughter? Has it really grasped that now, as never before, we have turned God's creatures into meat machines?

A few recent examples will suffice. During the last twelve months, unashamed, unabashed, and undaunted by criticism, the Church Commissioners have continued to allow hunting for sport and intensive farming on Church-owned lands.[1] The National Trust, to its credit, has at least had the courage to address the cruelty of deer hunting and take appropriate action;[2] not so the Commissioners. During the same period, one Anglican Cathedral sought to improve its finances by an auction of gifts—nothing wrong with that of course. It is when one discovers that one of the gifts was a free day's hunting with hounds that one begins to get disconcerted. Again, during this same period, a former Archbishop of Canterbury—the same one that came out publicly against factory farming when in office—went on record to defend intensive pig farming. He even spoke against, and voted in the House of Lords against, allowing pigs a few more inches of space because it was not "timely for the morale of those who have to look after them."[3] Being charitable is a challenge, so let me try: I do not think these bodies and individuals begin to understand the offence or the dismay that they provoke. The judgment of animal protectionists may sometimes be harsh, but the judgment of history will be even harsher.

Years ago, when I was a student in London, a group of us used to go to lectures in the Philosophy of Religion at Senate House. Somehow, we always used to end up at Tottenham Court Road underground station. I vividly remember that it had one quaint feature: a cranky old lift to the ground level. As we entered the lift, a mechanical voice used to repeat the words: "mind the gap." The phrase became a kind of mantra that entered into my soul. I do not think that the Church has begun to grasp the big gap, which is the credibility gap. Specifically, the gap between the Gospel it preaches and its practical insensitivity to cruelty. The Gospel is about the unlimited, free, generous love of God for creation—a generosity glimpsed in the life, passion, self-sacrifice, and death of Jesus Christ. The Gospel is the good news for the entire created order. God cares for each and every living creature. Not one sparrow is forgotten by God. If only ten percent of all that is true, then the Church should behave differently to animals.

People sometimes say to me, "Don't worry about the Church, Andrew; historically it has often been on the wrong

side. Just think about slavery, votes for women, capital punishment, or the rights of children. The Church has always led
from behind. In the end, it will give in to outside pressure and
support the animals' cause." Well, that does not please me. I
do not want the Church to support animals simply to conform
to secular pressure, rather I want the Church to see that its
own Gospel requires opposition to cruelty. What is needed is
for churches to see that their own doctrine of a loving, generous God requires us to act with costly generosity toward
animals. The challenge is for the churches to see what our
pioneering Christian forebears saw: cruelty is incompatible
with the Christian faith. As Anglican divine Humphry Primatt
wrote as early as 1776:

> We may pretend to what religion we please; but cruelty is athe-
> ism. We may make our boast of Christianity; but cruelty is
> infidelity. We may trust to our orthodoxy; but cruelty is the
> worst of heresies.[4]

Or they say: "Don't worry, Andrew, it is inevitable that the
Church should be predominantly, even overwhelmingly, concerned with human beings, and human interests, and human
welfare." Well, that does not gratify me. God is the Creator of
all creatures, not just human ones; there is something deeply
idolatrous in supposing that God is exclusively interested in
only one species among the millions that she has made. The
world looks in vain for Church leaders and theologians to
speak God's truth—that human interests are not God's only
interests in the world. The whole creation is not just made for
human betterment. God, not human beings, is the measure
of all things.

Again, they say: "Well, Andrew, you are a kind of prophet."
I am grateful for any kind words, and mostly they are indeed
well meant, but I am not interested in being a prophet. What
is needed is a prophetic Church. Most often I hear: "You need
to be patient, Andrew. The Church moves slowly; it takes
time, you can't expect the hierarchy to start taking up radical
positions." Well, I have been very patient—patient for more
than thirty years. If there are any brownie points for patience,

I have earned them all. Years ago, they called me an Angry Young Man. At least they cannot call me that anymore. Now, I am just an Angry Old Man. And as for radicalism, in all truthfulness, there is nothing more radical than the Christian Gospel. There is nothing more daring than the supposition that love will triumph over evil, that peace will overcome violence, and that even greedy, cruel, violent human beings will be redeemed.

Every year, I receive hundreds of letters from people deeply disillusioned with the Church's stance on animals. Some have already left or are on the way out. It is not difficult to know how they feel, but if all those who care for animals leave the Church, where will that leave the Church? It will leave the Church where for the most part it still is, on the wrong side of this debate. Of course, it is easy to moan about the Church. There will always be some enlightened bishops and Church leaders, and I thank God for them and pay tribute to them. But we cannot wait until the hierarchy comes to its senses; if we do that we shall be waiting until the Second Coming. No, we must begin now—after all, we are the assembled Church. The aim is to create an animal-friendly, animal-compassionate Church. And how do we do it?

This is my four-part strategy. *The first thing we need is an Animal Bible.* By that, I mean we need to draw out all those animal-friendly strands in scripture. Not everything in scripture is friendly either to animal rights or human rights. But what there is, is much friendlier than many suppose. Animal rightists have not invented the idea of universal peace wherein "the wolf lies down with the lamb" (Isaiah 11:6), neither have they invented the original divine command to be vegetarian (Genesis 1:29–30). Neither have we invented the idea of a covenant between God and all living creatures (Genesis 8:9–10), or dreamed up the covenant specifically with animals in which God will "abolish the bow, the sword, and war from the land" (Hosea 2:18). What we desperately need is a whole new generation of biblical scholars, exegetes, and interpreters who will give voice to these and the many other animal-friendly insights.

We must reject the "Bible bashers"—those people who use the Bible to beat up on animals. The Bible nowhere says that animals are just made for human use. It does not say that the whole earth is just ours to do with as we like. Neither does it say that God's sole interest is with the human species. We cannot allow such an important and influential book to become the preserve of those who want to exploit animals. The Bible needs to be read, studied, and reclaimed for the animals.

The second thing we need is Animal Theology. Theology was once defined by an Oxford undergraduate as "a way of bewildering oneself—methodically." Needless to say, I do not share that view. Theology is often described as something abstract, otherworldly, or simply theoretical, but in fact almost all the important reforming movements begin with some theology. As it has been said, there is nothing so practical as a good theory. We desperately need new theology that gives voice to the animals' cause. "History," it has been said, "is the province of the winners." But we must not allow the cause of justice for animals to be written out of Christian history. Who among Roman Catholics, for example, has ever heard of Cardinal Newman's doctrine of the Christ-like innocence of animals, and his view that the suffering inflicted upon innocent animals is morally equivalent to that inflicted on Christ himself?[5] Who among Methodists knows of John Wesley's detestation of blood sports and his defence of animal immortality?[6] Who among Anglicans knows that it was an Anglican priest, Arthur Broome, who founded the first animal protection society in the world, the RSPCA, in 1824?[7] That the system of anti-cruelty inspectors we know today was his vision and first financed out of his own pocket? Who among Evangelicals knows of William Cowherd, the former Swedenborgian minister, who founded the Bible-Christian Church in 1807?[8] This was the Church that made vegetarianism compulsory among its members, and which was the forerunner of the modern vegetarian movement.

The movement for the protection of animals has an honorable history with some of the greatest names of the Christian tradition to its credit, including William Wilberforce, John Wesley, C. S. Lewis—to take only three examples—but our story has yet to be fully told. In truth, it is hardly known. But there are signs of a new awakening. There are new books of creative theology now being published, like Stephen Webb's *On God and Dogs*,[9] John Eaton's *Circles of Creation*,[10] and Robert Murray's *The Cosmic Covenant*.[11] These books deserve to be powerfully supported and read. But we need not only books, but also a whole new generation of students, courses, research degrees, institutes, centers, and academies devoted to giving a new theological voice to animals. Already there is good news on the horizon. Hardly a week goes by without my receiving a letter from a student somewhere in the world interested in researching animal theology. We need to invest in the power of our ideas—in our theology—in order to create a better world for animals. The founding of the new Oxford Centre for Animal Ethics is an important step in that direction.

Thirdly, we need Animal Ministry. By that, I mean we need an uncompromising and robust understanding that it is a practical Christian duty to care for animals and alleviate their suffering. Platitudinous, lukewarm, half-hearted, half-baked ecclesiastical statements about animals will not suffice. If Christians believe in a ministry of reconciliation to all creatures, then we must mean business, and that means taking on business, specifically commerce that makes money out of animal misery.

So often Christians speak as if we are the "chosen species." I, for one, believe that we are the chosen species—not the master species but the servant species. Our vocation is to use our power for the weak, the defenseless, the vulnerable, the unprotected, and the innocent—precisely those who cannot represent themselves. That, for me, is Christian ministry: Christ-like ministry to *all* suffering creatures.

We desperately need a whole new generation of Christians, lay and ordained, who will grasp this issue of an inclusive ministry to all creation. Of course, we must be concerned with the salvation of human beings. Alone among creation, the human species is cruel, greedy, and sinful—we certainly need salvation. But animals need also to be saved from cruel, greedy, sinful human beings. Here is a whole new agenda for each national Church, and for every local church.

Finally, we need Animal Rites. So often Christian liturgy and worship are spiritually impoverished. We worship as if the world of creation was invisible. Worship should involve us in a celebration of all living creatures; it should invoke in us a sense of awe and wonder, and thanksgiving at God's magnificent world. Specifically, we need the liturgical means of celebrating the lives of animals, giving thanks for their companionship, praying for the relief of their suffering, and marking their death. My book *Animal Rites* is only one of many attempts and is only the beginning. But we must develop the task of turning around Christian liturgy so that it becomes animal-inclusive and animal-friendly. Here is an agenda for liturgists, poets, and hymn writers, to help Christian worship connect with the world of suffering creatures. That, then, should be our four-fold strategy. With the help of an Animal Bible, Animal Theology, Animal Ministry, and Animal Rites, we shall save the Church from its present spiritual blindness toward animals.

In a few moments, I am going to ask you to stand in silence to remember all those animals—hundreds, thousands, millions of them—who have died and suffered at human hands. We shall make a little history. It will be the first time that Christians have stood in a church and publicly commemorated the lives and deaths of God's other creatures. We do well to remember them.

Pope John Paul II is not my favorite theologian, but last March in the new Millennium, he did something courageous, even profound. He said sorry. He expressed his repentance for the sins of the Church—for example, in supporting anti-Semitism, in opposing women's rights, and in legitimizing violence against other believers.[12] There is always hope for a Church that repents. Let us hope that other Church leaders follow his example. Most of all, we need a Church that will publicly repent of its blindness and folly about animals, and especially its complicity in animal abuse and cruelty. God needs that Church and the animals need that Church. But it will not come without the work of many hands and much sacrificial effort, as well as the abundance of God's grace. I ask you to begin this task of renewal and reclamation with a simple, symbolic act of silent repentance.

God of Justice
fill us with
righteous anger
at the complacency
and callousness
of our lives.
God of mercy
drive from us
our hardness of heart
and renew your Spirit
of pity within us.
God of salvation
who redeems every creature
and whose triumph over death
is the hope of all creatures;
we remember before you
all those creatures
who have suffered and died
and we plead
for your mercy.
God of the universe
without boundaries
of race, creed, color, or species
in whose sight every life is precious;
send now your Spirit upon us
and liberate us
from that littleness
of mind, heart and soul
so that we may perceive
the kinship of all creatures,
and work towards that goal
in which all things
will be united in Christ. Amen.[13]

Appendix

An Open Letter to the Bishops on Hunting

The following is the text of a full-page advertisement, which appeared in the Church Times *(20 December 2002), sponsored by the Campaign to Protect the Hunted Animal, an umbrella group consisting of the League Against Cruel Sports, the International Fund for Animal Welfare, and the* RSPCA.

Dear Bishops,

Please forgive this unusual form of communication, but the matter has now become urgent, and there is little time left. The Government has now published its Bill on Hunting, and shortly both Houses in Parliament will have an opportunity to make their views known. I have read carefully the contributions made by the bishops in the Lords, and I believe that there are important theological and ethical considerations that have yet to be articulated.

The bishops who have spoken so far are concerned about the welfare of the rural communities they represent, and also about the social and cultural aspects of hunting. Some feel, quite understandably, that rural concerns have been marginalized, and that farmers are experiencing unique difficulties. It is less clear, however, that these bishops have heard those who regard the issue of cruelty as central to this debate. While some bishops have made references to animal welfare, very few have fully addressed the issue of cruelty.

I define "cruelty" as the deliberate infliction of suffering upon a sentient creature—when it is not performed for that individual animal's own benefit (for example, in a veterinary operation). That hunting with dogs is "cruel" is uncontestable. There is ample scientific evidence that all mammals experience stress, terror, shock, anxiety, fear, trauma, foreboding, as well as physical pain. It is also "deliberate" in that those who hunt do so with the express aim of pursuing a creature to its death. Not all may witness the death, but those who participate can be in no doubt about the result, at least, for most of the hunted species.

Humans are moral agents with the freedom to make moral decisions. That consideration is of central relevance to the debate about hunting. What is so objectionable is that moral beings, who should know better, choose to engage in an activity that results in cruelty. There is all the difference in the world between the accidental or instinctual infliction of harm by non-moral things or agents, and the volitional infliction of suffering by moral agents. In short: it is the difference between an "accident," or a "misfortune," and a morally evil act.

It therefore will not do, as some bishops have attempted, to justify hunting by reference to the facts that "foxes are not kindly in their ways," or that "the natural world is not a kindly place," as if nature was a moral textbook, or capable of relieving us of our obligations as moral agents. Strictly speaking, cruelty is a wholly human act; it presupposes freedom and intention.

There are good theological grounds for regarding such acts as intrinsically objectionable. Human beings are made in the "image of God" and given "dominion" over animals. It is true that, in the past, both notions have been used to defend an exploitative attitude toward animals, but there are almost no scholars today who endorse that implication. Rather, we are to act as God's deputies—made in the image of God who is holy, loving, and just, and uniquely commissioned to care for creation as God cares. To the question "Why should we care for animals?" there is only one biblical answer: "We are given that duty of care."

From this standpoint, the deliberate infliction of suffering on "lesser creatures" who are wholly in our power, and who are, strictly speaking, morally innocent, is a gross betrayal of our God-given responsibility. It is Christologically unenlightened for one bishop to defend hunting by arguing that "there is in the tradition of the three Abrahamic faiths a gulf fixed between the human race and the rest of the created order"—as if power was its own justification. That "gulf" should, at least in part, be filled up by the exercise of moral solicitude. As C. S. Lewis observed, our superiority over animals partly consists in our acknowledging obligations to them which they cannot acknowledge to us.

But cruelty is not just an intrinsically objectionable act; it is a token of moral meanness—a practical example of our failure to live generously after the example of Jesus. There is, as Cardinal Newman indicated, "something so very dreadful, so satanic in tormenting those who have never harmed us, and who cannot defend themselves, who are utterly in our power [and] who have weapons neither of offence or defence." And he concludes his consideration of the Christ-like innocence of animals with this appeal: "Think, then, my brethren of your feelings at cruelty practiced on brute animals, and you will gain one sort of feeling which the history of Christ's Cross and Passion ought to excite within you."

But there is more. Hunting is not undertaken (as all killing should be) as a regrettable act sometimes made necessary in a sinful and fallen world, rather it is celebrated as a "sport." It is here, most of all, that we should glimpse its utter incompatibility with the Gospel of God's free, generous love in Jesus Christ. People hunt because they enjoy it. In the words of Baroness Mallalieu: "Hunting is our music, it is our poetry, it is our art, it is our pleasure." Thousands have not marched in London simply to defend the "most efficient" means of killing foxes.

It is crucial to understand why the taking of pleasure in the infliction of suffering is so morally deplorable. It *may* be morally permissible to smack a child when performed with the intention of rectifying regressive behavior. But all should properly recoil at parents who *enjoy* this act. The taking of pleasure renders what might, conceivably, be a morally licit act into one that is disturbed, even depraved. A ban on hunting (any more than a ban on smacking) will not by itself prevent such depravity, but it will, at least, limit the number of victims.

Specifically, there is a Christian dimension, which deserves to be articulated. It is we—the species to whom so much power has been given—who should faithfully reflect that trust by acts of care and generosity to the animal world. If God's power in Christ was manifest in acts of sacrificial love, and a special solicitude exhibited towards the poor, weak, and vulnerable, should not our power be so similarly directed? And are all those Christian virtues to be solely exercised in relation to ourselves?

I fear not only the judgment of God, but also the judgment of history. Is hunting now to be counted among the long list of moral issues, including capital punishment, votes for women, or the protection of children, on which bishops have either frustrated, or voted against, reform? There is no more desultory experience than reading the past record of Anglican bishops on moral issues.

Specifically, it is odd to see bishops so apparently uncomprehending of the anti-cruelty cause, since our Christian forebears pioneered it. Many luminaries of the nineteenth century—William

Wilberforce, Lord Shaftesbury, and Fowell Buxton, to take only three examples—saw it as their Christian duty to oppose cruelty in all its forms. Anglican priest Arthur Broome founded the SPCA (as it then was) in 1824 as a Christian organization.

In 1909, the Bishop of Hereford sponsored—with the support of five other members of the bench of bishops—a bill to outlaw deer hunting, pigeon shooting, and rabbit coursing. Speaking in support, the then Archbishop of Canterbury commented that "I firmly believe that fifty years hence it will be found as impossible for the then members of your Lordships' House to realize why we refrained from taking exception to rabbit-coursing as it is pursued today as we now find it difficult to understand why a hundred years ago exception was not taken to things like bull-baiting." Almost one hundred years later, it appears that the sensibilities of (at least the most vocal) Christian bishops are no more advanced about hunting and coursing than they were about bull-baiting. The hunting debate is at a critical juncture. The Government is now proposing a fudged piece of legislation, which will allow the hunting of foxes, mink, and hares to continue under license. Licensing will imbue these "sports" with a kind of legitimacy that they do not possess morally and ought not to have legally. Indeed, the whole notion of "licensing" cruel acts is an affront to moral theology. The so-called principles of "utility" and "cruelty" (like the question-begging formula "necessary cruelty") presuppose a wholly utilitarian (and secular) justification for cruelty. There are times when some measure of compromise may be morally laudable, but this is not one of them. Hunting mammals with dogs for sport belongs to that class of always morally impermissible acts, along with rape, child abuse, and torture. Whatever else is true, the Christian Gospel and cruelty are incompatible. In the debates so far, the bench of bishops have voted for the continuance of hunting. But I do not believe that these bishops represent the mind of the Church in England, or of the wider Anglican Church in this country. I appeal to those many bishops who are opposed to hunting, whether in the Lords or not, to make their voices known—and I would be grateful to hear from them. It would be tragic if the Church utterly wrongfooted itself in this debate to which it has so much to contribute.

I wish you—and all God's creatures—a peaceful Christmas.

—Andrew Linzey

Guide to Further Reading

The following are some of the major books on religion and animals.

Akers, Keith, *The Lost Religion of Jesus: Simple Living and Non-violence in Early Christianity* (New York: Lantern Books, 2000). The foreword is by Professor Walter Wink. A provocative work that argues that Jesus was an "Ebionite," committed to non-violence to animals and humans. Many will find the thesis problematic, but it is argued with lucidity and scholarship.

Anon, *The Animals' Lawsuit Against Humanity: A Modern Adaptation of an Ancient Animal Rights Tale* (Louisville, Kentucky: Fons Vitae, 2005). Tr. and adapted by Anson Laytner and Dan Bridge, edited by Matthew Kaufman, introduced by Seyyed Hossein Nasr, and illustrated by Kulsum Begum. This tale has a remarkable history. Various versions of the story circulated by word of mouth, but the first written version appeared in Arabic, composed by members of the Islamic "Order of the Pure Brethren," a Sufi order (possibly in Iraq), sometime during the tenth century. Much later, it was translated by Rabbi Kalonymus ben (son of) Kalonymus, known among Christians as Maestro Calo, at the request of his master, the French King Charles of Anjou, in 1316. The tale must be one of the first texts to deploy sophisticated theological arguments against human maltreatment of animals.

Armstrong, Susan J., and Richard G. Botsler (eds), *The Animal Ethics Reader* (London and New York: Routledge, 2003). An admirable and comprehensive anthology of 588 pages that is set to become a major course text. Its section on religious perspectives is unduly modest with only five essays (by Norman Soloman, Stephen Fuchs,

Martin Forward, Michael W. Fox, and myself), but this could be rectified in future editions.

Bekoff, Marc with Carol Meaney (eds), *Encyclopaedia of Animal Rights and Animal Welfare* (Westport: Greenwood Press, 1998). Foreword by Dr. Jane Goodall. This comprises a range of theological topics, including "Animal theology," "*Theos*-rights," Theodicy," "Reverence for life," and numerous short biographies of formative religious thinkers written by myself.

Berry, R. J. (ed.), *The Care of Creation: Focusing Concern and Action* (London: Inter-Varsity Press, 2000). Foreword by John Stott. This is a collection of responses to the *Evangelical Declaration on the Care of Creation* (1994). Sadly, the book wholly reflects the deficiencies of the Declaration in failing to recognize animals as an issue of moral concern or even opposing the deliberate infliction of cruelty. It is a palpable sign of the ecological myopia when it comes to animals found in conservative evangelical work. For a critical review, see Andrew Linzey, *Third Way*, 23/6 (July 2000), 23–25.

Birch, Charles and Lukas Vischer, *Living with the Animals: The Community of God's Creatures* (Geneva: WCC Publications, 1997). This comprises two essays, one exploring the biblical material and the other examining the Christian tradition. A short, but impressive introduction to the subject.

Carpenter, Edward, "Christian Faith and the Moral Aspect of Hunting" in Patrick Moore (ed.), *Against Hunting* (London: Gollancz, 1965). The groundbreaking essay by the former Dean of Westminster that challenged traditional thinking about animals.

Chapple, Christopher Key, *Nonviolence to Animals, Earth, and Self in Asian Traditions* (Albany: State University of New York Press, 1993). A sensitive exploration of the theme of non-violence in Asian religious traditions. Succinct and comprehensive.

Clark, Stephen R. L., *The Moral Status of Animals* (Oxford: The Clarendon Press, 1977). An admirable and wide-ranging philosophical discussion, which holds that "this at least cannot be true, that it is proper to be the cause of avoidable ill" (Preface). It contains insightful discussions of religious and theological viewpoints.

Dombrowski, Daniel A., *Hartshorne and the Metaphysics of Animal Rights* (Albany: State University of New York Press, 1988). A pioneering work based on the process theology of Charles Hartshorne who wrote the groundbreaking article on "The Rights of the Subhuman World," *Environmental Ethics*, 1 (1979), 49–60.

Eaton, John, *The Circle of Creation: Animals in the Light of the Bible* (London: SCM Press, 1995). A readable, introductory account of animal-friendly teaching in scripture. Eaton's lightness of touch masks considerable biblical scholarship.

Edwards, Denis, *Jesus: The Wisdom of God: An Ecological Theology* (Minneapolis: St. Paul's, 1995). One of the few ecotheological works that expressly includes sentient creatures within its purview. It draws on the notion of Jesus as the embodiment of Hebrew Wisdom tradition. An admirable and, sadly, much neglected work of creative theology.

Fern, Richard L., *Nature, God and Humanity: Envisioning an Ethics of Nature* (Cambridge: Cambridge University Press, 2002). A remarkably muddled and incoherent account of our moral obligations to creation, and especially to animals. The following is typical: "What advocates of vegetarianism tend to overlook, understandably, being that they are vegetarian, is the extent proposals for the abandonment of meat-based foods threaten the general sense of wellbeing on which every society depends" (p. 239). Such wide claims, without sufficient argumentation, must be treated as suspect.

Galloway, Allan, *The Cosmic Christ* (London: Nisbet & Sons, 1951). Sadly long out of print, it hasn't been bettered as a systematic study. It makes the overwhelmingly convincing case that the work of Christ is effective for all creation. An essential corrective to contemporary humanocentric perspectives.

Grant, Robert M., *Early Christians and Animals* (London and New York: Routledge, 1999). This is an utterly frustrating volume mostly consisting of lengthy extracts of works by the Alexandrians, the Antiochenes, the Latin Fathers, and Isidore of Seville, without any introductions, notes, or discussions of their relevance. A deeply disappointing work by a New Testament scholar, who could have helped us understand the place of animals in the often confusing world of the first three centuries. For a critical review, see Andrew Linzey, *Church Times* (10 December 1999), 10.

Kalechofsky, Roberta (ed.), *Judaism and Animal Rights: Classical and Contemporary Responses* (Marblehead: Micah Publications, 1992). This is indispensable reading for the range of Jewish views on the status of animals.

Linzey, Andrew, *Animal Rights: A Christian Assessment* (London: SCM Press, 1976). The first modern work on the status of animals from a Christian standpoint, it critiques the traditional criteria for rights (personhood, rationality, soul possession) as inadequate and proposes sentiency as an alternative criterion. It argues, among other things, that the humanocentricity of traditional perspectives is spiritually impoverished and theologically inexcusable.

Linzey, Andrew, *Christianity and the Rights of Animals* (London: SPCK, and New York: Crossroad, 1987). This provides a new conception of rights, based on the rights of the Creator to have what is created treated with respect. It argues that all sentient creatures have "*theos*-rights" and are subjects of intrinsic value. The first systematic attempt to relate the notion of animal rights to biblical insights and to provide a theological grounding for the rights of the creature.

Linzey, Andrew and Tom Regan (eds), *Animals and Christianity: A Book of Readings* (London: SPCK, and New York Crossroad, 1988). The first anthology of Christian texts on animals, with extracts from partisans on both sides of the debate, including Aquinas, Augustine, Karl Barth, Bonaventure, Calvin, Descartes, Irenaeus, Thomas More, Albert Schweitzer, Tolstoy, and Wesley. It includes a General Introduction, "The Great Ethic," pp. ix–xv, and five sectional introductions based on issues in the texts: "Attitudes to Creation," "The Problem of Pain," The Question of Animal Redemption," "Reverence, Responsibility and Rights" and "Practical Issues." The book was reissued in 2007 by Wipf and Stock, of Eugene, Oregon.

Linzey, Andrew, *Animal Theology* (London: SCM Press, and Chicago: University of Illinois Press, 1994). This is the most comprehensive treatment of the status of animals from a theological perspective. It argues, among other things, that human dominion over animals "needs to take as its model the Christ-given paradigm of lordship manifest in service," p. ix.

Linzey, Andrew and Dan Cohn-Sherbok, *After Noah: Animals and the Liberation of Theology* (London: Mowbray, now Continuum, 1996). The first comprehensive study of Jewish and Christian teaching about animals, which shows the resources within both traditions for a positive understanding of animals. The final chapter, "How animals can liberate Jewish and Christian theology," pp. 117–37, demonstrates how animals raise fundamental questions about our understanding of God, and why religion needs to give attention to animals in order to save itself from Feuerbach's charge of deifying the human species.

Linzey, Andrew and Dorothy Yamamoto (eds), *Animals on the Agenda: Questions about Animals for Theology and Ethics* (London: SCM Press, and Chicago: University of Illinois Press, 1998). This is the most comprehensive collection of original studies on animals and theology ever published, with contributions by Richard Bauckham, J. W. Rogerson, Stephen R. L. Clark, John B. Cobb Jr., Michael

Lloyd, Paul Badham, J. B. McDaniel, Walter Houston, John Muddiman, Thomas E. Hosinski, and others. It contains my Foreword, pp. ix–x, my Introductory essay, "Is Christianity Irredeemably Speciesist?" pp. xi–xx, and four sectional introductions, "Understanding Scriptural Perspectives," pp. 3–7; "Wrestling with the Tradition," pp. 63–66; "Disputed Questions" pp. 115–19, and "Obligations to Animals" pp. 203–205.

Linzey, Andrew, *Animal Gospel: Christian Faith as if Animals Mattered* (London: Hodder and Stoughton, and Louisville, Kentucky: Westminster John Knox Press, 1999). This is an evangelical sequel to *Animal Theology*, which argues, among other things, that there is something Christ-like about the innocent suffering of animals, which should compel a response of Christ-like generosity.

Linzey, Andrew, *Animal Rites: Liturgies of Animal Care* (London: SCM Press, and Cleveland, Ohio: The Pilgrim Press, 1999). This includes fourteen new liturgies, including services celebrating animal companionship, services for animal welfare, healing liturgies, new eucharistic prayers "for the whole creation," and animal burial services to enable Christian communities to celebrate animals as God's creatures and our relationship with them. There is a lengthy introduction, titled "Not A Sparrow Falls: Reclaiming Animal-Friendly Spirituality," pp. 1–21.

Linzey, Andrew and Paul Barry Clarke (eds), *Animal Rights: A Historical Anthology* (New York: Columbia University Press, 2005). This is a collection of more than fifty extracts showing how thought about animals, and our duties toward them, has been a concern of philosophers, political theorists, and theologians as diverse as Plato, Aquinas, Descartes, Hobbes, Kropotkin, John Stuart Mill, Karl Marx, and Albert Schweitzer. It contains the Editors' Introduction on how the circle of justice may yet be widened to include animals, pp. xiii–xxii.

McDaniel, Jay B., *Of God and Pelicans: A Theology of Reverence for Life* (Louisville, Kentucky: Westminster John Knox Press, 1989). This is a pioneering attempt by a process theologian to employ the insights from Schweitzer's philosophy to illuminate creation and animal issues. His subsequent *Earth, Sky, Gods, and Mortals: Developing an Ecological Spirituality* (Mystic: Twenty-Third Publications, 1990) is an excellent course text, setting out the issues for students and teachers.

Murray, Robert, *The Cosmic Covenant: Biblical Themes of Justice, Peace and the Integrity of Creation* (London: Sheed and Ward, 1992). This is a highly accomplished examination of the biblical material; Chapter 6 in particular develops a very strong argument drawn from the kingship tradition with respect to animals. A painstaking and groundbreaking work by a Jesuit scholar, it has been sadly neglected.

Phelps, Norm, *The Dominion of Love: Animal Rights According to the Bible* (New York: Lantern Books, 2002). This is an impressive introductory work, which uses biblical scholarship to make a succinct theological case for animals.

Pinches, Charles and Jay B. McDaniel (eds), *Good News for Animals? Christian Approaches to Animal Well-Being* (Maryknoll: Orbis Press, 1993). This is a pioneering anthology (now sadly out of print) based on the conference at Duke University in 1990, which was one of the first to bring together serious theological voices for animals. Pinches' provocative essay "Each According to Its Kind: A Defense of Theological Speciesism," (pp. 187–205) awaits a thoughtful, theological response.

Primatt, Humphry, *The Duty of Mercy and the Sin of Cruelty to Brute Animals* [1776], edited by Richard D. Ryder (Fontwell: The Centaur Press, 1992). The Preface is by Bishop John Austin Baker. Primatt's insistence on the incompatibility of Christianity with cruelty makes this a landmark work.

Regan, Tom (ed.), *Animal Sacrifices: Religious Perspectives on the Use of Animals in Science* (Philadelphia: Temple University Press, 1986). Introduced by Professor John Bowker, *Animal Sacrifices* is a pan-religious anthology with some groundbreaking essays. James Gaffney's piece on "The Relevance of Animal Experimentation to Roman Catholic Ethical Methodology" is admirable for its insights and lucidity. It also contains my essay on "The Place of Animals in Creation—A Christian View."

Robson, Michael, *St. Francis: The Legend and the Life* (London: Geoffrey Chapman, 1997). This is one of the best lives of St. Francis, which combines scholarship and insight and which does not overlook his radical view of creation and animals in particular. In the light of these works on St. Francis, it is difficult to know why so many Franciscans still specifically shun concern for animal welfare as a Christian issue.

Salisbury, Joyce E., *The Beast Within: Animals in the Middle Ages* (London and New York: Routledge, 1994). This reinforces a rather bleak view of the Middle Ages as one with precious little sympathy for animals and their proper treatment. It is difficult to exonerate the churches for culpability in that regard since they were perhaps the major intellectual influence of the period.

Sapontzis, Steve F. (ed.), *Food for Thought: The Debate over Eating Meat* (Amherst: Prometheus Books, 2004). This comprises essays for and against, including essays on the religious aspect by John Berkman, Roberta Kalechofsky, Tom Regan, James Gaffney, and myself. An excellent course text for students and teachers.

Schochet, Elijah J., *Animal Life in Jewish Tradition* (New York: K'tav, 1984). This is a monumental and comprehensive source book for Judaism and animals. A classic work.

Schwartz, Richard H., *Judaism and Vegetarianism* (New York: Lantern Books, 2001). This shows, among other things, how the biblically based Jewish injunction *tsa'r ba'alei chayim* (not to cause pain to any living creature) justifies a thoroughgoing vegetarianism. A classic work. Also of interest is his *Judaism and Global Survival* (New York: Lantern Books, 2002), which makes the case for vegetarianism based on concerns about world hunger.

Schweitzer, Albert, *Civilisation and Ethics*, tr. by C. T. Campion (London: Allen & Unwin, 1923). Schweitzer is still the neglected figure in Christian writing on animals, especially since he anticipated both animal and ecological sensitivity. Despite all its theological limitations, *Civilisation and Ethics* is still an inspiring and deeply moving account of his conception of "reverence for life."

Simoons, Frederick J., *Eat Not This Flesh: Food Avoidances from Prehistory to the Present* [1961] (Madison: University of Wisconsin Press, second edition, 1994). This is a generally comprehensive work on the theory and practice of food restrictions, but it is rather limited in its grasp of moral and specifically religious considerations.

Sorrell, Roger D., *St. Francis of Assisi and Nature: Tradition and Innovation in Western Christian Attitudes toward the Environment* (New York: Oxford University Press, 1988). This is a scholarly analysis of the long tradition of concern for nature within Christianity. It also shows how Francis's view of creatures was anticipated by earlier saints.

Tillich, Paul, "Nature, Also, Mourns for a Lost Good" in *The Shaking of the Foundations* (New York: Scribners, 1962). A much-neglected essay illustrates both Tillich's concern for nature and his theological grasp of the ambiguity of nature.

Walters, Kerry S. and Lisa Portmess (eds), *Religious Vegetarianism from Hesiod to the Dalai Lama* (Albany: State University of New York Press, 2001). This is a useful anthology that provides readings from Pythagorean, Indian, Buddhist, Jewish, Christian, and Islamic traditions on vegetarianism. An excellent course text.

Webb, Stephen H., *On God and Dogs: A Christian Theology of Compassion for Animals* (New York: Oxford University Press, 1998).

Foreword by Andrew Linzey. This is an insightful and creative work, which focuses on companion animals as bearers of God's grace.

Wennberg, Robert N., *God, Humans and Animals: An Invitation to Enlarge Our Moral Universe* (Grand Rapids: William B. Eerdmans, 2003). A rather disturbing book that concludes that "God permits animal pain and suffering for human advantage, that is, as part of the context for human soul-making and decision-making" (p. 339). Again: "These creatures have their own value and significance, but their pain and suffering may be permitted (in part) as a means to create lovers, worshippers, and glorifiers of God. . . . That is to say that the permitted pain and suffering is for divine advantage" (p. 340). One wonders whether there is a doctrine of a just God, or any God worth the name, that is rescuable from such a cruel hypothesis. Wennberg also misperceives my theory of "*theos*-rights," claiming that I place it in juxtaposition with Tom Regan's own secular theory (which I do not) (p. 167). There is no essential contradiction in holding that animals have inherent value and that that value is upheld by God the Creator whose creatures they are.

Young, Richard Alan, *Is God a Vegetarian?* (New York: Open Court Publishing, 1999). Despite the unfortunate title, this is actually a serious evangelical discussion of the biblical basis for vegetarianism by an American theologian.

Notes

Introduction

1. See Andrew Linzey, "Introduction," *Christianity and the Rights of Animals* (London: SPCK, and New York: Crossroad, 1987), pp. 1–6.
2. One remarkable book in this regard is Charles Birch's *Feelings* (Sydney: University of New South Wales, 1995), which explores the "feelings" of human beings, nature, animals, and God. Birch is a professor of biology who harmonizes biological and theological perspectives and has done so excellently in this book. A scholarly and deeply imaginative work that has been much neglected.
3. See, for example, *The Dictionary of Ethics, Theology and Society* which I co-edited with Paul Barry Clarke (London and New York: Routledge, 1996); P. A. B. Clarke and Andrew Linzey, *Research on Embryos: Politics, Theology and Law* (London: LCAP, 1988), and, more recently, *Gays and the Future of Anglicanism*, which I co-edited with Richard Kirker (Winchester, UK, and New York: O Books, 2005).
4. See Andrew Linzey, *Public Morality and the Canadian Seal Hunt* (London: Respect for Animals, and Washington: The Humane Society of the United States, 2005).
5. I have made this point at length in *Christianity and the Rights of Animals*, pp. 147–149, and in many subsequent writings.
6. *Christianity and the Rights of Animals*, pp. 100f.
7. Andrew Linzey, "Truth and Reconciliation," *The Animals' Agenda*, 19/1 (January/February, 1999), 19.
8. Taken from Andrew Linzey, "Putting Our House in Order," *The Animals' Agenda*, 21/5 (September/October 2001), 21. See also my earlier protests: Andrew Linzey, "On Lions and Lambs: Why

Violence in Pursuit of Animal Rights is Morally Self-contradictory," *The Times Higher Education Supplement* (9 February 1994), 21, and Andrew Linzey, "Dear Animal Rights Activist," *The Independent* (4 November 1994), 21.

  9. See Martin Hugh, *The Pankhursts* (London: Allen Lane, 2001). See, for example, on p. 243, where the wave of attacks on property made parliamentarians reverse their support for the Conciliation Bill of 1912 that extended suffrage. This is only one of many examples in this fine, instructive study.
 10. Andrew Linzey, "Putting Our House in Order," p. 21.

1: Religion and Sensitivity to Animal Suffering

  1. Sydney Evans, *Prisoners of Hope*, edited by Brian Horne and Andrew Linzey (Cambridge: Lutterworth Press, 1990), p. 101.
  2. Cited in *The Beginning*, the history of the World Congress by Marcus Braybrooke, <www.worldfaiths.org/Beginning.htm>.
  3. Andrew Linzey and Dan Cohn-Sherbok, *After Noah: Animals and the Liberation of Theology* (London: Mowbray, now Continuum, 1997), p. 12.
  4. Schweitzer popularized the term, and actually claimed it as his own, but arguably borrowed it from Hindu and Jain traditions, see Ara Barsam, *Reverence for Life: Albert Schweitzer's Great Contribution to Ethics* (New York: Oxford University Press, 2008).
  5. See Andrew Linzey, *Animal Theology* (London: SCM Press, and Chicago: University of Illinois Press, 1994), Chapter 3, "Humans as the Servant Species," for supporting discussion, pp. 45–61.
  6. William James, "The Philosopher and the Moral Life" in *The Will to Believe, and Other Essays in Popular Philosophy* (New York: Dover, 1956), p. 211; cited and discussed in Gerald E. Myers, *William James: His Life and Thought* (New Haven and London: Yale University Press, 1986), pp. 446f.
  7. Jonathan Edwards, *Charity and Its Fruits* (Edinburgh: Banner of Truth Trust, 1969), pp. 157–158; cited and discussed in James M. Gustafson, *Theology and Ethics* (Oxford: Basil Blackwell, 1981), pp. 305f.
  8. Treaty of Amsterdam 1997. Protocol on improved protection and respect for the welfare of animals. The Treaty agreed in June 1997 was officially signed by the Member States of the European Union on 2 October 1997, and entered into force on 1 May 1999. I am grateful to Wendy Smith for this reference.

9. "Pampering the Pets, and Then Some," *Zenit, Weekly News Analysis: The World Seen From Rome* (5 June 2004), 6.
10. Andrew Linzey, *Animal Rites: Liturgies of Animal Care* (London: SCM Press, and Cleveland, Ohio: The Pilgrim Press, 1999), p. 109.
11. "Hunt enthusiasts call faithful to Free Church of Country Sports," *Sunday Times* (23 May 2004).
12. For a discussion, see Andrew Linzey, *Christian Theology and the Ethics of Hunting with Dogs* (London: Christian Socialist Movement, 2003).
13. William Godwin, *Enquiry Concerning Political Justice and Its Influence on Modern Morals* [1798] (London: J. Watson, 1842), p. 217, extract in Andrew Linzey and P. A. B. Clarke (eds), *Animal Rights: A Historical Anthology* (New York: Columbia University Press, 2005), pp. 132–134.

2: Theology As If Animals Mattered

1. Karl Barth, *Church Dogmatics*, 3/2, *The Doctrine of God*, edited by G. W. Bromiley and T. F. Torrance (Edinburgh: T. & T. Clark, 1960), p. 6.
2. Barth, *Church Dogmatics*, 3/4, *The Doctrine of Creation*, edited by G. W. Bromiley and T. F. Torrance (Edinburgh: T. & T. Clark, 1961), p. 333. My critique and attempted reconstruction of Barth can be found in Andrew Linzey, "The Neglected Creature: the Doctrine of the Non-Human Creation and its Relation to the Human in the Thought of Karl Barth," Ph.D. dissertation, University of London, 1986.
3. Aristotle, *The Politics* (Harmondsworth: Penguin Books, 1985) tr. by T. A. Sinclair, revised by T. J. Saunders, p. 79.
4. Thomas Aquinas, "Summa Contra Gentiles" in Anton C. Pegis (tr.), *Basic Writings of Saint Thomas Aquinas* (New York: Random House, 1945), 2: 221; extract in Andrew Linzey and P. A. B. Clarke (eds), *Animal Rights: An Historical Anthology* (New York: Columbia University Press, 2005), p. 10.
5. *Catechism of the Catholic Church* (London: Geoffrey Chapman, 1994), para 299, p. 71 and para 2415, p. 516; my emphases.
6. Gerd Lüdemann, *The Unholy in Holy Scripture: The Dark Side of the Bible* (London: SCM Press, 1996), translated by John Bowden. This is a disturbing and important book that explores genocide and anti-Judaism in scripture.

7. Joseph Rickaby, *Moral Philosophy* (London: Longman, 1901), "Ethics and Natural Law," 2: 199.

8. James M. Gustafson, *Theology and Ethics* (London: Blackwell, 1981), p. 112.

9. Christina Rossetti, from "To What Purpose This Waste?" anthologized in Jon Wynne-Tyson, *The Extended Circle: A Dictionary of Humane Thought* (Fontwell: The Centaur Press, 1985), p. 281.

10. Athanasius, *Contra Gentes and De Incarnatione*, ed. and tr. by R. W. Thompson (Oxford: The Clarendon Press, 1971), p. 115.

11. Ludwig Feuerbach, *The Essence of Christianity*, ed. and tr. by George Eliot, Introduction by Karl Barth, Foreword by H. Richard Niebuhr (New York and London: Harper Torchbook, 1957); see especially p. xix, cited and discussed in Andrew Linzey and Dan Cohn-Sherbok, *After Noah: Animals and the Liberation of Theology* (London: Mowbray, now Continuum, 1997), p. 119f.

12. Brian L. Horne, *Imagining Evil* (London: Darton, Longman and Todd, 1996), pp. 130–131, cited together with my response in Andrew Linzey, "C. S. Lewis's Theology of Animals," *Anglican Theological Review*, 80/1 (Winter 1998), 71.

13. Andrew Linzey, *Animal Theology* (London: SCM Press, and Chicago: University of Illinois Press, 1994), p. 71. For Keith Ward's translation and paraphrase of the Old Testament, see *The Promise* (London: SPCK, 1980), p. 2.

14. Andrew Linzey, *Animal Rites: Liturgies of Animal Care* (London: SCM Press, and Cleveland, Ohio: The Pilgrim Press, 1999), "Celebrating the Creatures: A Liturgy," pp. 28–29.

15. Charles Péguy, cited in Alan Ecclestone, *Yes to God* (London: Darton, Longman and Todd, 1975), p. 121; original source not supplied.

16. I have adapted the last three paragraphs from my *Animal Gospel: Christian Faith As If Animals Mattered* (London: Hodder and Stoughton, and Louisville, Kentucky: Westminster John Knox Press, 1999), pp. 5–6.

3: Animal Rights and Animal Theology

1. Joseph Kirwan, "Greens and Animals" in Robert Whelan, Joseph Kirwan, and Paul Haffner, *The Cross and the Rain Forest: A Critique of Radical Green Spirituality* (Grand Rapids, Michigan: W. B. Eerdman, 1996), pp. 112–13, 122.

2. Friedrich Wilhelm Nietzsche, "Schopenhauer as Educator" [1874] in *Thoughts Out of Season*, tr. by Adrian Collins (Edinburgh: T. N.

Foulis, 1909), Part II, pp. 149–155; extract in Andrew Linzey and P. A. B. Clarke (eds), *Animal Rights: A Historical Anthology* (New York: Columbia University Press, 2005), p. 148.

3. Michel Eyquem Montaigne, "Apology for Raymond Sebound" [ca.1592] in *Essays of Montaigne*, tr. by E. J. Trechman (London: Oxford University Press, 1927), p. 452; extract in *Animal Rights*, p. 65.

4. Lord Shaftesbury, Letter, 30 April, 1881, cited and discussed in Andrew Linzey, *Animal Theology* (London: SCM Press, and Chicago: University of Illinois Press, 1994), p. 36f.

5. Alexander Pope, "Of Cruelty to Animals" [1713] in Rosalind Wallace (ed.), *A Hundred English Essays* (London: Thomas Nelson, 1950), pp. 159–65; extract in *Animal Rights*, p. 72.

6. Richard French, *Anti-Vivisection and Medical Science in Victorian England* (Princeton, New Jersey: Princeton University Press, 1975), p. 35.

7. Cardinal Heenan, Foreword to Ambrose Agius, *God's Animals* (London: Catholic Study Circle for Animal Welfare, 1970), p. 2.

8. Andrew Linzey, *Christianity and the Rights of Animals* (London: SPCK, and New York: Crossroad, 1987), p. 97.

9. Kirwan, "Greens and Animals," p. 105.

10. The argument is outlined in "The Moral Priority of the Weak," Chapter Two of *Animal Theology*, pp. 28–44.

4: The Conflict between Ecotheology and Animal Theology

1. See "Points of Religious Agreement in Environmental Ethics," <www.wildbirds.org/info/religion.htm>. The summary is the result of research by Kusumita P. Pedersen, "Environmental Ethics in Interreligious Perspective," in Sumner B. Twiss and Bruce Grelle (eds), *Explorations in Global Ethics: Comparative Religious Ethics and Interreligous Dialogue* (Oxford: Westview Press, 1998), and is reprinted on the web with permission of Libby Bassett, John T. Brinkman, Kusumita P. Pedersen (eds), *Earth and Faith* (New York: United Nations Environment Programme, 2000), p. 78.

2. Annie Dillard, *Pilgrim at Tinker Creek* [1975], Introduction by Richard Adams (London: Pan Books, 1976), unattributed cover blurb.

3. Dillard, p. 154.

4. Dillard, p. 157.

5. Dillard, p. 158.

6. Dillard, p. 231; original emphases.
7. Dillard, p. 237.
8. Richard Adams, Introduction, Dillard, p. 9.
9. Richard Cartwright Austin, *Beauty of the Lord: Awakening the Senses* (Atlanta: John Knox Press, 1988), pp. 196–97. Both this passage and the following one from Matthew Fox, as well as my prefacing comments, are cited and discussed in Andrew Linzey, *Animal Theology* (London: SCM Press, and Chicago: University of Illinois Press, 1994), p. 119.
10. Matthew Fox, *Original Blessing* (Santa Fe: Bear and Company, 1983). Fox's conclusions logically follow from his rejection of the fallenness of creation.
11. Matthew Fox in Matthew Fox and Jonathon Porritt, "Green Spirituality" [interview], *Creation Spirituality*, 8/3 (May–June, 1991), 14–15, and in *Animal Theology*, pp. 119–22.
12. For an important discussion of this question, see Stephen R. L. Clark, "Is Nature God's Will?" in Andrew Linzey and Dorothy Yamamoto (eds), *Animals on the Agenda: Questions about Animals for Theology and Ethics* (London: SCM Press, and Chicago: University of Illinois Press, 1998), pp. 123–36.
13. Jay B. McDaniel, "Can Animal Suffering be Reconciled with Belief in an All-Loving God?" in Linzey and Yamamoto, *Animals on the Agenda*, p. 163.
14. McDaniel, in Linzey and Yamamoto, *Animals on the Agenda*, p. 168.
15. "There was also a failure to face up to the realities of the natural world as revealed by biologists and others." From a review of my *Animal Theology* by C. S. Rodd, *The Expository Times*, 106/1 (October, 1994), 4. It is a charge, of course, to which I gladly plead guilty. All Christian theology has to some degree, as Karl Barth once noted, to be logically inconsequent in the face of the facts, or rather some facts.
16. Friedrich Wilhelm Nietzsche, "Schopenhauer as Educator" [1874] tr. by Adrian Collins, *Thoughts Out of Season* (Edinburgh: T. N. Foulis, 1909), Part II, p. 149; extract in Andrew Linzey and P. A. B. Clarke (eds), *Animal Rights: An Historical Anthology* (New York: Columbia University Press, 2005), p. 148.
17. Nietzsche, *Thoughts Out of Season*, p. 54, and in *Animal Rights*, pp. 151–52.
18. Martin Luther, *Lectures on Romans*, edited by William Pauck (London: SCM Press, 1961), Library of Christian Classics, 15: 237.

19. Schelling cited in Paul Tillich, "Nature, Also, Mourns for a Lost Good" in *The Shaking of the Foundations* (New York: Scribners, 1962), p. 83.
20. Tillich, *The Shaking of the Foundations*, p. 81.
21. E. L. Mascall, *The Christian Universe* (London: Darton, Longman and Todd, 1966), p. 163f. Mascall's thesis of the progressive "Christification" of the natural order has been overlooked by theologians.
22. Tillich, *The Shaking of the Foundations*, p. 86.
23. For my work on Barth, see Andrew Linzey, "The Neglected Creature: The Doctrine of the Human and its Relationship to the Non-Human in the Thought of Karl Barth," Ph.D. Dissertation, University of London, 1986. Barthian themes also emerge in Andrew Linzey, *Christianity and the Rights of Animals* (London: SPCK, and New York: Crossroad, 1987).
24. Albert Schweitzer, *Civilisation and Ethics* [1923], tr. by C. T. Campion (London: Allen and Unwin, 1967), p. 216. For a full-length treatment, see Ara Barsam, *Reverence for Life: Albert Schweitzer's Great Contribution to Ethics* (New York: Oxford University Press, 2008).
25. Anne Primavesi, *From Apocalypse to Genesis: Ecology, Feminism and Christianity* (Minneapolis: Fortress Press, 1991), p. 146. For a critical review, see Andrew Linzey, *Scottish Journal of Theology*, 45/2 (1992), 265–266.
26. See, for example, my debate with Hugh Fearnley-Whittingstall, "Should We All Be Vegetarians?" *The Ecologist*, 34/8 (October, 2004), 23–27. Although Fearnley-Whittingstall is not a theologian, he reflects much of eco-thought by not seeing a "moral" problem about killing.
27. Stephen R. L. Clark, *The Moral Status of Animals* (Oxford: The Clarendon Press, 1977), p. 183.
28. C. S. Lewis, *Present Concerns*, edited by Walter Hooper (New York: Harcourt Brace Jovanovich, 1986), p. 79; cited and discussed in Wesley A. Kort, *C. S. Lewis: Then and Now* (New York: Oxford University Press, 2001), p. 156. See also my extensive discussion on the value of Lewis' thought, Andrew Linzey, "C. S. Lewis's Theology of Animals," *Anglican Theological Review*, 80/1 (Winter, 1998), 60–81.
29. *Animal Theology*, pp. 90–91.
30. Bishop of Bath and Wells (Jim Thompson), *Hansard*, 623/45 (12 March 2001), col. 537. See my response, Andrew Linzey,

"An Open Letter to the Bishops on Hunting," *Church Times*, 20/27 (December, 2002), 10; reproduced as an Appendix.

31. Archbishop John Habgood, *Hansard*, 623/45 (12 March 2001), col. 611.

32. Edward Carpenter, "Christian Faith and the Moral Aspect of Hunting" in Patrick Moore (ed.), *Against Hunting* (London: Gollancz, 1965), p. 137. For my discussion, see Andrew Linzey, *Christian Theology and the Ethics of Hunting with Dogs* (London: Christian Socialist Movement, 2003), pp. 1–24.

33. Communication from DEFRA to the author, 18 October 2004. For my critique of the concept of biodiversity and the way in which it is used to justify killing, see Andrew Linzey, "Against Biodiversity," *The Animals' Agenda*, 21/2 (March/April 2001), 21.

34. Communication from DEFRA, 18 October 2004.

35. Communication from DEFRA to the author, 10 August 2004. The scientific work that forms the basis of the Government's case can be found, among other things, in J. M. Rhymer and D. D. Simberloff, "Extinction by Hybridisation and Introgression," *Ann. Rev. Ecol. Syst.* (1996) 17: 83–109. But, like most scientific work, it fails to question underlying assumptions about the relative value of genetic purity, extinction and welfare.

36. The answer from DEFRA is that "a range of control measures have been tested and the most effective identified [i.e. shooting]," Communication from DEFRA, 18 October 2004. But this rush to the gun must be questioned. Why should not taxpayers' money be spent on morally preferable options, even if they yield slower results, especially since total eradication is a near-impossibility?

37. In particular, Animal Aid has led a valiant fight against the slaughter, see <www.animalaid.org.uk/campaign/wildlife/ruddycull.htm>.

38. Communication from DEFRA, 18 October 2004.

39. Communication from DEFRA, 18 October 2004.

40. Communication from DEFRA, 18 October 2004.

41. Communication from DEFRA, 18 October 2004; my emphasis.

5: Responding to the Debate about Animal Theology

1. Robert Murray, *The Cosmic Covenant: Biblical Themes of Justice, Peace and the Integrity of Creation* (London: Sheed and Ward, 1992).

2. See, for example, Cassandra Williams, "Andrew Linzey's Animal Theology and the Educational Ministry of the Christian Church," Ph.D. Dissertation, Presbyterian School of Christian Education, Virginia (Michigan: UMI Dissertation Service, 1998), which analyzes and critiques my use of scripture.

3. See Andrew Linzey, "The Neglected Creature: The Doctrine of the Non-Human and its Relationship to the Human Creation in the Work of Karl Barth," Ph.D. Dissertation, University of London, 1986.

4. See, for example, the argument of John Woolman (1720–1772) in his early statement on slavery: "The parent of mankind is gracious: his care is over smallest creatures; and a multitude of men escape not his notice: and though many of them are trodden down, and despised, and yet he remembers them: he sees their affliction, and looks upon the spreading increasing exaltation of their oppressor," *Some Considerations on the Keeping of Negroes*, 1754 and 1762, in Mason Lowance (ed.), *Against Slavery: An Abolitionist Reader* (Harmondsworth: Penguin Books, 2000), p. 23 [language modernized]. In other words, it is the graciousness or generosity of God, disclosed in Jesus, which makes oppression intolerable.

5. Andrew Linzey, Introduction to "Understanding Scriptural Perspectives" in Andrew Linzey and Dorothy Yamamoto (eds), *Animals on the Agenda: Questions about Animals for Theology and Ethics* (London: SCM Press, and Chicago: University of Illinois Press, 1998), p. 3; original emphasis.

6. These texts, and many others, are discussed in Andrew Linzey and Dan Cohn-Sherbok, *After Noah: Animals and the Liberation of Theology* (London: Mowbray, now Continuum, 1997), pp. 17–34.

7. There are both positive and negative Christian and Jewish traditions about animals, but Judaism is noteworthy in advancing the principle that unnecessary suffering should not be inflicted on animals, a principle which was later adopted by Christians, specifically those who founded the first SPCA, see *After Noah*, p. 9f.

8. Pope John Paul II, *Div. et Red.* 50; recently discussed in Edward P. Echlin, "Christian Ecology for Today," *Social Justice Newsletter*, 64 (October, 2003), 11f.

9. Andrew Linzey, *Animal Theology* (London: SCM Press, and Chicago: University of Illinois Press, 1994), pp. 57 and 123.

10. I have made the logic of this clearer in Andrew Linzey, "Unfinished Creation: The Moral and Theological Significance of the Fall," *Ecotheology*, 4 (January, 1998), 20–26. In my view, much ecotheology issues in a non-redeeming God and therefore a non-God, at least as traditionally understood.

11. *Animal Theology*, p. 120.

12. See Andrew Linzey, "C. S. Lewis' Theology of Animals," *Anglican Theological Review*, 80/1 (Winter, 1998), 60–81.

13. See, for example, Andrew Linzey, "Animal Rights: A Reply to Barclay," *Science and Christian Belief*, 5/1, 47–51, and Andrew Linzey, "For Animal Rights" and "Linzey's Reply," in Michael Leahy and Dan Cohn-Sherbok (eds), *The Liberation Debate: Rights at Issue* (London and New York: Routledge, 1996), pp. 171–87 and 205–207.

14. After *Animal Rights: A Christian Assessment* (1976), the important works are: *Christianity and the Rights of Animals* (1987), *Compassion for Animals* (1988), *Animals and Christianity: A Book of Readings* (1989), *Political Theory and Animal Rights* (1990), *Animal Theology* (1994), *After Noah* (1997), *Animals on the Agenda* (1998), *Animal Gospel* (1999) and *Animal Rites: Liturgies of Animal Care* (1999).

15. On sentiency, see, for example, Andrew Linzey, *Christianity and the Rights of Animals* (London: SPCK, and New York: Crossroad, 1987), pp. 77–86.

16. Andrew Linzey, "Is Christianity Irremediably Speciesist?," Introduction to *Animals on the Agenda*, p. xvii.

6: Jesus and Animals: A Different Perspective

1. Translation of Coptic text in Richard Bauckham, "Jesus and Animals I: What did he Teach?" in Andrew Linzey and Dorothy Yamamoto (eds), *Animals on the Agenda: Questions about Animals for Theology and Ethics* (London: SCM Press, and Chicago: University of Illinois Press, 1998), (hereafter Bauckham), pp. 38–39; also cited and discussed in Andrew Linzey and Dan Cohn-Sherbok, *After Noah: Animals and the Liberation of Theology* (London: Mowbray, now Continuum, 1987), p. 66f.

2. Roderick Dunkerley, *Beyond the Gospels* (London: Penguin Books, 1957), p. 143.

3. Bauckham, p. 39.

4. Bauckham, p. 29.

5. The Protoevangelium of James, para 18:1, in J. K. Elliott (ed.), *The Apocryphal New Testament: A Collection of Apocryphal Christian Literature in an English Translation based on M. R. James* (Oxford: The Clarendon Press, 1993), p. 64.

6. Elliott, p. 49.

7. Song of Anna, para 3:1, Elliott, p. 58.

8. Elliott, p. 58.

9. The Infancy Gospel of Thomas, para 2:1 (Greek A version) in Elliott, pp. 75–76.

10. Elliott, p. 68.

11. Elliott, p. 69.

12. See Elliott, paras 16:1 (Greek A), 1 (Latin), 2 (Latin), pp. 79–83.

13. The Gospel of Pseudo-Matthew, para 14, in Elliott, p. 94.

14. Wilhelm Schneemelcher (ed.), edited and tr. by R. McL. Wilson, *New Testament Apocrypha*, 1: *Gospels and Related Writings* (Cambridge: James Clarke, and Louisville, Kentucky: Westminster John Knox Press, 1991), p. 65.

15. Elliott, p. 95.

16. Elliott, p. 95.

17. Elliott, pp. 97–98.

18. For Aquinas on how we can have "no friendship with irrational creatures," see *The Summa Theologica* of St. Thomas Aquinas, translated by Fathers of the English Dominican Province (New York: Benzinger Bros, 1918), Part 1, Questions 6.41 and 65.3; extract in Andrew Linzey and P. A. B. Clarke (eds), *Animal Rights: A Historical Anthology* (New York: Columbia University Press, 2005), pp. 102–105. For a discussion of St. Francis of Assisi in comparison with St. Thomas, see Andrew Linzey and Ara Barsam, "St. Francis of Assisi" in Joy A. Palmer (ed.), *Fifty Key Thinkers on the Environment* (London and New York: Routledge, 2001), pp. 22–27.

19. William Morrice, *Hidden Sayings of Jesus: Words Attributed to Jesus Outside the Four Gospels* (London: SPCK, 1997) p. 143; my emphasis. Morrice's criteria for determining authenticity strike me as entirely subjective and question-begging, pp. 17–23.

20. Christopher R. Matthews, "Articulate Animals: A Multivalent Motif in the Apocryphal Acts of the Apostles," in Francois Bovon, Ann Graham Brock, and Christopher R. Matthews (eds), *The Apocryphal Acts of the Apostles*, Harvard Divinity School Studies (Cambridge: Harvard University Press, 1999), p. 232. Matthews says of the Apocryphal Acts that they represent "certain

strands of early Christian optimism [that] saw them [animals] awash in human salvation," (p. 205), but I would also want to add that whatever instrumentalist tendencies are present, they also offer an inclusive vision of both animal and human redemption.

7: Animals and Vegetarianism in Early Chinese Christianity

1. Martin Palmer, *The Jesus Sutras: Rediscovering the Lost Religion of Taoist Christianity* (London: Piatkus Publishing, 2001), verses 3:54–55 and 3:70–73, p. 223; my emphases.
2. Palmer, 7:34, p. 67.
3. Palmer, 1:11, p. 139.
4. Palmer, 4:20, p. 164.
5. Palmer, 5:15, p. 166.
6. Palmer, 5:41 and 5:46, pp. 167–68; my emphasis.
7. See also Ray Riegert and Thomas Moore, *The Lost Sutras of Jesus*, translated by Jon Babcock (London: Souvenir Press, 2004).
8. Palmer, p. 253.
9. Palmer, 1:3 and 1:15, pp. 159–60.
10. Palmer, 2:15–17, p. 57.
11. Palmer, 2:6, p. 140.
12. Palmer, 3:16, p. 149.
13. The Gospel of the Ebionites, from Epiphanius, adv. Haer., paras 30.13, 30.16 and 30.22, cited and discussed in J. K. Elliott (ed.), *The Apocryphal New Testament: A Collection of Apocryphal Christian Literature in an English Translation based on M. R. James* (Oxford: The Clarendon Press, 1993), pp. 15–16. See my discussion of these texts making some of the same points, and nine other apocryphal texts, in <www.godandanimals.com/PAGES/linsey/apocry.html>.
14. Keith Akers, *The Lost Religion of Jesus: Simple Living and Nonviolence in Early Christianity* (New York: Lantern Books, 2000), p. 26. The Foreword is by Professor Walter Wink.
15. Richard Baukham, "Jesus and Animals II: What did he Practise?" in Andrew Linzey and Dorothy Yamamoto (eds), *Animals on the Agenda: Questions about Animals for Theology and Ethics* (London: SCM Press, and Chicago: University of Illinois Press, 1998), pp. 49–60. Baukham's work repays careful study, but one is left with a paradox: Jesus apparently taught kindness to animals and fulfills Jewish messianic hopes,

including an endorsement of the "original vegetarianism of all living creatures," but was not himself a vegetarian and even personally sacrificed animals at the Temple. If that is true, it is difficult, among other things, to account for both the traditions of Christian vegetarianism and the fact that the early Church effectively abolished animal sacrifices (see my critique, pp. 3–7).

16. Robert Eisenman, *James, the Brother of Jesus: Recovering the True History of Early Christianity*, 1: *The Cup of the Lord* (London: Faber & Faber, 1997), see pp. 258–390.

17. Roger T. Beckwith, "The Vegetarianism of the Therapeutae, and the Motives for Vegetarianism in Early Jewish and Christian Circles," *Revue de Qumran*, 13/49–52 (October, 1988), 409. I am grateful to Roger Beckwith for this reference and for other insights.

18. See, for example, Philip Kapleau, *To Cherish All Life: The Buddhist Case for Vegetarianism* (Rochester: The Sen Center, 1986), p. 29f, and Bodhin Kjolhede, "The Buddhist Case for Vegetarianism" in Andrew Linzey (ed.), *The Encyclopaedia of Global Animal Concern*. And for a seminal work on *ahimsa*, see Christopher Key Chapple, *Nonviolence to Animals, Earth, and Self in Asian Traditions* (Albany: State University of New York Press, 1993).

19. Some of the non-violent and compassionate themes that emerge from a study of Asian theology are explored in Choan-Seng Song, *Theology from the Womb of Asia* (London: SCM Press, 1988). But, despite the author's admirable concern with creation and ecological issues, the tradition of vegetarianism and non-violence to animals is entirely overlooked.

8: On Being an Animal Liturgist

1. Unknown source cited by Archbishop Robert Runcie, "Theology, the University and the Modern World," in P. A. B. Clarke and Andrew Linzey (eds), *Theology, the University and the Modern World* (London: LCAP, 1988), p. 20; original emphasis.

2. Louis Bouyer, *Rite and Man: The Sense of the Sacral and Christian Liturgy*, tr. by M. Joseph Costelloe (London: Burns and Oates, 1963), p. 9; cited and discussed in Andrew Linzey, *Animal Rites: Liturgies of Animal Care* (London: SCM Press, and Cleveland, Ohio: The Pilgrim Press, 1999), p. 14.

3. *Animal Rites*, p. 15.

4. Joseph Kirwan, "Greens and Animals" in Robert Whelan, Joseph Kirwan, and Paul Haffner (eds), *The Cross and the Rain Forest: A Critique of Radical Green Spirituality* (Grand Rapids, Michigan: William B. Eerdmans, 1996), p. 111.

5. For example, Andrew Linzey, *Christianity and the Rights of Animals* (London: SPCK, and New York: Crossroad, 1987).

6. Richard Curtis and Paul Mayhew-Archer, *The Vicar of Dibley: The Great Big Companion to Dibley* (London: Michael Joseph, 2000) p. 84. I acknowledge my indebtedness to these fine writers who have helped put both Dibley and animal services on the map.

7. Vincent van Gogh, cited in Mark Roskill (ed.), *The Letters of Van Gogh* (London: Fontana, 1982), p. 124; cited and discussed in Andrew Linzey, *Animal Gospel: Christian Faith as if Animals Mattered* (London: Hodder and Stoughton, and Louisville, Kentucky: Westminster John Knox Press, 1999), p. 173–74.

8. *Catechism of the Catholic Church* (London: Geoffrey Chapman, 1994), p. 517, para 2418. In order to understand this odd comment, one needs to appreciate that for centuries it was standard Catholic teaching that one had no duty to love animals—a view that stemmed expressly from St. Thomas Aquinas, see my chapter 7, "Why Church Teaching Perpetuates Cruelty," *Animal Gospel*, pp. 64–72. Although slighting, it actually represents an advance on the previous position.

9. Stephen H. Webb, *On God and Dogs: A Christian Theology of Compassion for Animals* (New York: Oxford University Press, 1998), p. 6.

10. Arthur Broome, "Prospectus of the SPCA," RSPCA Records, 2 (1823–1826). I am grateful to the Librarian of the RSPCA for this reference.

11. Lambeth Conference 1998, Resolution 1.8 Creation (a) (iii), cited and discussed in *Animal Rites*, p. 108. The resolution is as follows: "This Conference: (a) reaffirms the Biblical vision of Creation according to which: Creation is a web of inter-dependent relationships bound together in the Covenant which God, the Holy Trinity has established with the whole earth and every living being. (i) the divine Spirit is sacramentally present in Creation, which is therefore to be treated with reverence, respect, and gratitude; (ii) human beings are both co-partners with the rest of Creation and living bridges between heaven and earth, with responsibility to make personal and corporate sacrifices for the common good of all Creation; (iii) the redemptive pur-

pose of God in Jesus Christ extends to the whole of Creation."
This is a remarkably adroit theological statement and deserves
to be more widely known. See <www.anglicancommunion.org/
lambeth/1/sect1rpt. html>.

12. Prayers from "A Liturgy for Animal Burial," *Animal Rites*, pp.
113–14.
13. For a helpful survey and discussion of the various models of animal redemption, both individual and corporate, see Petroc and
Eldred Willey, "Will Animals be Redeemed?" in Andrew Linzey
and Dorothy Yamamoto (eds), *Animals on the Agenda: Questions
about Animals for Theology and Ethics* (London: SCM Press,
and Chicago: University of Illinois Press, 1994), pp. 190–200.
My own view is that all sentient beings will be redeemed in a
way that compensates them for the injustice and suffering that
they have had to undergo. That I believe is required by the doctrine of a just God. *How* precisely that will be done, I am happy
to leave to the Almighty.
14. Allan Galloway, *The Cosmic Christ* (London: Nisbet & Sons,
1951), p. x. He convincingly argues that much of the cosmic
imagery of the New Testament was designed to "symbolise all
the distortion in the structure of existence" on one hand, and
to assert "that the work of Christ is universally effective for
all creation," on the other. The doctrine of the cosmic Christ
"arose as a necessary implication of the fundamental insights of
Jewish and Christian theology," pp. 28, 29, 55.
15. Prayers from "A Liturgy for Animal Burial," *Animal Rites*, p.
110–11.
16. Prayers from "Celebrating the Creatures: A Liturgy," *Animal
Rites*, pp. 28–30.
17. "Pet's Death Inspires Liturgies for Animals," *The Washington
Post*, 3 March, 1999. Among the many other reports (which
seemed to go on for a year) both satirical and serious, see:
"They Are God's Best Friends Too; Ben Fenton on the Theolo-
gians Who Believe Heaven Would Be Hell without Dogs," *The
Daily Telegraph* (18 September 1999); Robbie Millen, "Barking
Dogma," *The Spectator* (18 September 1999); "Will Your Pet
Rise Again? Yes, Some Faiths Say," *The Philadelphia Inquirer*
(7 February 1999); "Do Dogs Go to Heaven?; *Los Angeles Dog
Fancy Magazine* (September 1999), 25–28; "Animals in the
Afterlife," *Charleston Post and Courier* (10 February 1999);
"'I Totally Believe in Animals in Heaven,' Says Animal Rights
Theologian," Press release, *Ecumenical News International* (8

March 1999); "God Loves Animals Too," *Christian Herald* (7 April 1999); "Tail-Wagging Theology," *Reform* (magazine of the United Reformed Church) (April 1999).

18. "Sittichs Seele: Der british Theologe hat ein Gebetbuch geschrieben, das der Menschheit noch fehlte: eins für die Tiere," *Der Spiegel "Special"* 7 (1999). See also "Ein Gebetbuch für Tiere: Anglikanischer Priester sorgt mit Werk für Aufregung," *Blick In Die Welt* (18 April 1999).

19. "Nee, de doop voor dieren is niet nodig," *Trouw* (Dutch daily newspaper) (4 August 1999), 12.

20. The initial press report, "Prayer Book for Pets Launched," *The Independent* (29 January 1999), was followed by an interview with Paul Vallely, "The Lord Is My Shepherd," *The Independent* (3 February 1999).

21. Quoted in *The Washington Post* (3 March 1999).

22. "For Pets We See No Longer," *Church Times* (29 January 1999). There was also a page devoted in the same issue to an interview with Margaret Duggan, "Talking of Animals," p. 12.

23. Andrew Linzey, "Franciscan Concern for Animals" in Damian Kirkpatrick, Philip Doherty, and Sheelagh O'Flynn (eds), *Joy in All Things: A Franciscan Companion* (Norwich: The Canterbury Press, 2002), pp. 68–72.

24. "The Lord Is Your Pet's Shepherd Also. . . ." *Irish Independent* (18 February 1999).

25. *Irish Independent* (18 February 1999).

26. "Pets in the Pew," *The Tablet* (6 February 1999).

27. Review of *Animal Rites*, in *Liturgy: Journal of the Catholic Bishops; Conference of England and Wales* (1999), 180–81.

28. *Catholic Catechism*, p. 69, para 294. I accept, however, that the *Catechism* tends towards a very humanocentric view of redemption, which I think is the result of a failure to grasp the significance of the Logos doctrine at this point, see pp. 68–76. It quotes Bonaventure, for example, on how God created all things "not to increase his glory but to show it forth and to communicate it" (pp. 68–69), but fails to acknowledge that Bonaventure saw *all* creatures as icons of Christ: "For every creature is by its nature a kind of effigy and likeness of the eternal Wisdom," "The Soul's Journey into God," *Bonaventure*, tr. and introduction by Ewert Cousins, Preface by Ignatius Brady (*Classics of Western Spirituality*, London: SPCK, 1978), p. 77; my emphasis.

29. C. N. Cochrane, *Christianity and Classical Culture: A Study in Thought and Action from Augustus to Augustine* (London:

Oxford University Press, 1944), pp. vi and 238; my emphases. This is a vital work for understanding the development of the Logos doctrine.

30. A. N. Wilson, "Diary," *New Statesman* (5 February 1999), see also <www.newstatesman.com/199902050005>.
31. "In Dog We Trust," *Mail on Sunday* (7 March 1999).
32. "Pandora," *The Independent* (11 February 1999).
33. Review of *Animal Rites* by Michael J. Townsend, *The Expository Times* (Spring, 1999), 120.
34. Review of *Animal Rites* by Martyn Gross, *Crucible* (Journal of the Board for Social Responsibility of the Church of England) (January/March, 2000), 150–53.
35. Comments that appear on the back cover of *Animal Rites*.
36. *A Service for Animal Welfare* can be obtained from the RSPCA, Wilberforce Way, Southwater, Horsham, West Sussex RH13 9RS, telephone +44 ⁰870 3335 999, or online at<www.rspca. org.uk>.
37. This story originally appeared in my article on animal services in the *Church Times* (1 October 2004). The following week a letter was published from a clergyman in Yorkshire who was also a member of the National Ferret Welfare Society. He was indignant: "I was disappointed to read in the first paragraph of what was otherwise a very good article . . . the usual negative image of ferrets and their owners. The popular misconception that ferrets are small, smelly animals that bite and are to be found down the trousers of foolish men is very wrong indeed. A ferret is no more likely to bite than any other small mammal, and is, in fact, an attractive, curious and friendly creature. Ferret-owners are by no means all uncouth, vulgar people. I have kept ferrets for many years, and have never yet been bitten or uttered profanities at the altar rail." This was an absolutely fair admonition, and I apologize for any offence. I, too, think highly of ferrets, and I hope the author will agree with me that it is a terrible shame that such a creature is also used to hunt and terrorize rabbits—a practice which I have seen first hand and which is frankly beyond the pale.
38. Albert Schweitzer, *Civilisation and Ethics*, tr. by C. T. Campion, London: Allen & Unwin, 1923, p. 119.

9: Summing Up: Towards a Prophetic Church for Animals

1. The Church Commissioners manage the finances of the Church of England, including land owned by the Church. Their official

and long standing policy on fox-hunting is that "our tenants should follow their own consciences in deciding whether or not to allow hunts on the land we entrust to their care," "Policy on Fox-Hunting" (London: Church Commissioners, March 1992). Despite many protests, they maintained this position up to the abolition of hunting with hounds in 2004. Instead of providing a moral lead to the nation, they had, in the end, to simply follow public opinion embodied in legislation. A missed opportunity, to say the least. For my account of one attempt in General Synod to influence the policy of the Commissioners, see Andrew Linzey, "Cruelty in the Church's Own Backyard," Chapter 14, *Animal Gospel: Christian Faith as if Animals Mattered* (London: Hodder and Stoughton, 1999), pp. 130–39. This chapter does not appear in the US edition of the book (published by Westminster John Knox) because of its specifically UK focus.

2. The National Trust commissioned a Report by Professor Patrick Bateson, Provost of King's College, Cambridge, and the Biological Secretary of the Royal Society, into the suffering caused by deer hunting. Bateson concluded that hunted deer experience a level of suffering comparable to that sustained by an animal that loses a limb in a road accident. (Patrick Bateson, FRS, *Behavioural and Physiological Effects of Culling Red Deer, Report to the Council of the National Trust*, March 1997). After these findings were published, the Trust decided not to permit deer hunting with hounds on its land.

3. "Robert Runcie, the former amateur pig breeder and professional Archbishop of Canterbury, has set aside ecclesiastical cares to speak up for Britain's hard-pressed pig farmers. Writing in today's *Telegraph*, he accuses rich animal welfare pressure groups of ignorance about farm conditions, and denounces as a 'travesty' the treatment of British farmers in their struggle against their European competitors. Of the pressure groups, he writes that few people today have any direct contact with farm animals, 'Yet many have strong views about how they should be treated and feel qualified to dictate to those who have their daily care and management.'" See "Runcie Attacks 'Ignorant Critics of Pig Farming,'" *The Daily Telegraph* (6 March 2000). In the same issue is an article by Runcie titled "Support the Stockman—He Knows What's Best for His Pigs." Runcie spoke against Lord Beaumont's Welfare of Pigs Bill, which, among other things, proposed more space and improved bedding, as well as limits to tail docking, *Hansard* (House of Lords) (26

January 2000), col. 75. (The statement in the text appears in col. 77). All this might seem unexceptional given that Church leaders are so infrequently heard in the cause of animal welfare, except that it is difficult to reconcile at least with the spirit of his previous statement against intensive farming when he was Archbishop of Canterbury: "Many have written to me on the subject of hens in battery cages and veal calves in crates. Of course, these systems of extreme confinement are to be abhorred. . . . As a practical pig farmer I have found it possible to keep my pigs in conditions which respect their natural sphere of existence. I derive pleasure from seeing their response to this more humane treatment and I am sure that other stockmen feel the same towards their animals in similar circumstances. . . ." "Statement by the Archbishop of Canterbury on Factory Farming" (London: Lambeth Palace, 1981), extract in Andrew Linzey, *Christianity and the Rights of Animals* (London: SPCK, and New York: Crossroad, 1986), "Appendix: Church Statements on Animals, 1956–1986," p. 155.

4. Humphry Primatt, *The Duty of Mercy and the Sin of Cruelty to Brute Animals* [1776], edited by Richard D. Ryder (Fontwell: The Centaur Press, 1992), p. 125. The Preface is by Bishop John Austin Baker. Primatt's work was foundational to the emergence of the animal protection movement. Arthur Broome, who founded the SPCA (as it then was) in 1824, published an abridged version of Primatt's work in 1831 (p. 11 in Ryder's Introduction).

5. "I mean consider how very horrible it is to read the accounts which sometimes meet us of cruelty inflicted on brute animals. For what was this but the very cruelty inflicted upon our Lord?," John Henry Newman, "The Crucifixion" [1842] Sermon X, *Parochial and Plain Sermons* (London: Rivingtons, 1868), pp. 133–45. See also my discussion, "The Christ-like Innocence of Animals," Chapter 8, *Animal Gospel*, pp. 73–77.

6. See Andrew Linzey, "John Wesley—An Early Prophet of Animal Rights," *The Methodist Recorder* (10 April 2003), 15. For his sermon on animal immortality, see John Wesley, *Sermons on Several Occasions*, 4 Vols with biographical note by J. Beecham (London: Wesleyan Conference Office, 1874). Vol. ii contains his sermon "The General Deliverance," pp. 121–32, in which he espouses animal immortality. For Wesley's opposition to cruel sports, see his entry for July 1756, *Journal* (standard edition) (London: Charles H. Kelley, 1909), 4: 176.

7. Arthur Broome called the first meeting to inaugurate the Society. His work was immensely sacrificial. He gave up his London church to work full-time (unpaid) for the Society as its first Secretary, and ended up in prison because of the Society's debts. See James Turner, *Reckoning with the Beast: Animals, Pain, and Humanity in the Victorian Mind* (Baltimore and London: Johns Hopkins University Press, 1980), pp. 40–44.

8. The Church was founded in Salford in 1807. One of Cowherd's followers, William Metcalfe, subsequently traveled to America and became one of the "greatest advocates of vegetarianism the nation has ever known," Karen Iacobbo and Michael Iacobbo, *Vegetarian America: A History* (Westport, Connecticut: Praeger Publishing, 2004), p. 11. See my "Foreword: Veggie Pilgrim Fathers," pp. ix–xi. The Iacobbos' book is a remarkable history of vegetarianism and its religious and theological history. See, also, the *History of the Bible-Christian Church, 1817–1817* (Philadelphia: J. B. Lippincott Company, 1922), which provides a detailed account of how Bible-Christians lived and fared in carnivorous America. I am grateful to Bernard Unti for this reference.

9. Stephen H. Webb, *On God and Dogs: A Christian Theology of Compassion for Animals* (Oxford: Oxford University Press, 1998). Foreword by Andrew Linzey, pp. ix–xii.

10. John Eaton, *The Circle of Creation: Animals in the Light of the Bible* (London: SCM Press, 1995).

11. Robert Murray, *The Cosmic Covenant: Biblical Themes of Justice, Peace, and the Integrity of Creation* (London: Sheed and Ward, 1992).

12. "At a solemn service of penance in St. Peter's Basilica in Rome, Pope John Paul II made history on March 12 by begging pardon of God for the sins committed by members of his Church over the past 2,000 years, especially those that caused division among Christians. At the same time the pope reaffirmed the sanctity of 'Mother Church.' The document [*Memory and Reconciliation: The Church and the Faults of the Past*] on which the confession is based stresses that while the Church always remains holy, its members can make mistakes," *The Christian Century* (22 March 2000). So it appears that the document acknowledges sins only by those acting in the *name of the Church*, rather than any sins *by the Church itself*, or those who have served as its popes. My tribute should therefore be quali-

fied. See Andrew Linzey, "Why We Should Applaud Pope John Paul II," *Church of England Newspaper*, 8 July 1999, p. 21.

13. The prayer is taken from Andrew Linzey, *Animal Rites: Liturgies of Animal Care* (London: SCM Press, 1999, and Cleveland: Ohio: The Pilgrim Press, 2000), p. 130.